GROUP PORTRAIT
HOTOGRAPHY HANDBOOK

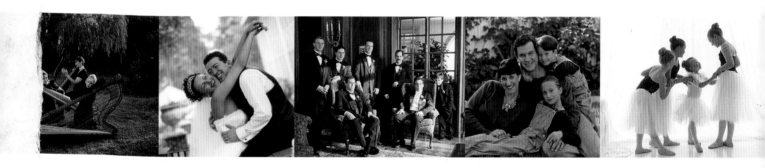

ILL HURTER

MHERST MEDIA, INC. ■ BUFFALO, NY

Photos by: J. J. Allen, Michael J. Ayers, Vladimir Bekker, David Bentley, Anthony Cava, Stephen Dantzig, Terry Deglau, William L. Duncan, Gary Fagan, Rick Ferro, Frank A. Frost, Dale P. Hansen, Robert L. Kunesh, Robert Lino, Robert Love, Suzanne Love, Heidi Mauracher, William S. McIntosh, Andy Park, Richard Pahl, Norman Phillips, Stephen Pugh, Patrick Rice, Kimarie Richardson, Kenneth Sklute, David Anthony Williams, and Monte Zucker.

Front cover photograph courtesy of Frank A. Frost. Back cover photograph by Stephen Pugh. Diagrams courtesy of Norman Phillips. Diagrams drawn by Shell Dominica Nigro.

Published by:
Amherst Media, Inc.
P.O. Box 586
Buffalo, N.Y. 14226
Fax: 716-874-4508
www.AmherstMedia.com

Publisher: Craig Alesse
Senior Editor/Production Manager: Michelle Perkins
Assistant Editor: Barbara A. Lynch-Johnt

ISBN: 1-58428-082-4
Library of Congress Control Number: 2001133135

Printed in Korea.
10 9 8 7 6 5 4 3 2 1

TABLE OF CONTENTS

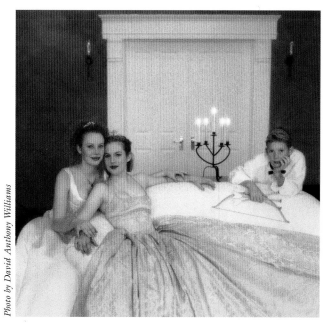

Photo by David Anthony Williams

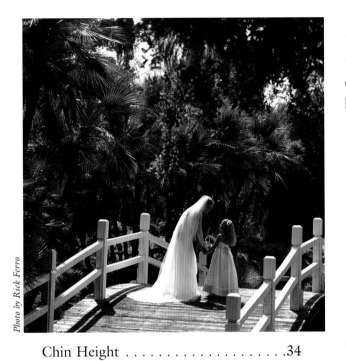

Photo by Rick Ferro

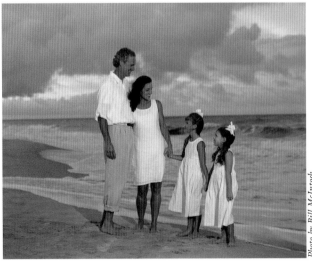

Photo by Bill McIntosh

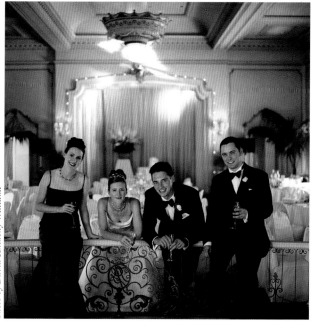

Photo by David Anthony Williams

CHAPTER 6

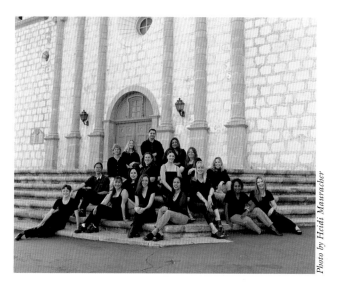

Photo by Heidi Mauracher

Introduction

Any time you try to pose two or more people in a photograph and render them looking happy and relaxed, you'll understand why professional portrait photographers are so well paid. Photographing portraits of groups is not easy.

Many group portraits are family portraits—records of happiness and togetherness. Taken every few years, the family portrait provides cherished memories of how the family looked "back then" and a fond record of the children's growth.

Family groups taken in the home show the familiar warmth of home and according to many, probably bring the largest economic return. Outdoor family portraits are a close second, with the studio portrait usually ranking last in terms of popularity and sales.

When and why do people have a family portrait made? Master photographer Robert Love says, "In our area, the number one reason that clients call us to create a family portrait is because the complete family is getting together for a special occasion. Usually the parents have one or more grown children who don't live at home anymore. More often than not, this person is married and has a family, as well. Now we have an opportunity to create a third generation memento. With these extended families, we have photographed from eight to thirty people in one image."

A group portrait is only as good as each of the individuals in the portrait. You should be able to look at each person in the portrait and ask, "Could each of these individual portraits stand alone?" If the answer is "Yes," then the photographer has done a good job.

A group portrait is only as good as each of the individuals in the portrait.

According to one of the great group portrait photographers, Monte Zucker, "The first thing to remember is that each person in the group is interested primarily in how he or she looks. So, that means that you have to pay attention to each and every person in the group, individually. No matter how good the pattern of the group, if people don't like the way they look, all your time and effort are wasted."

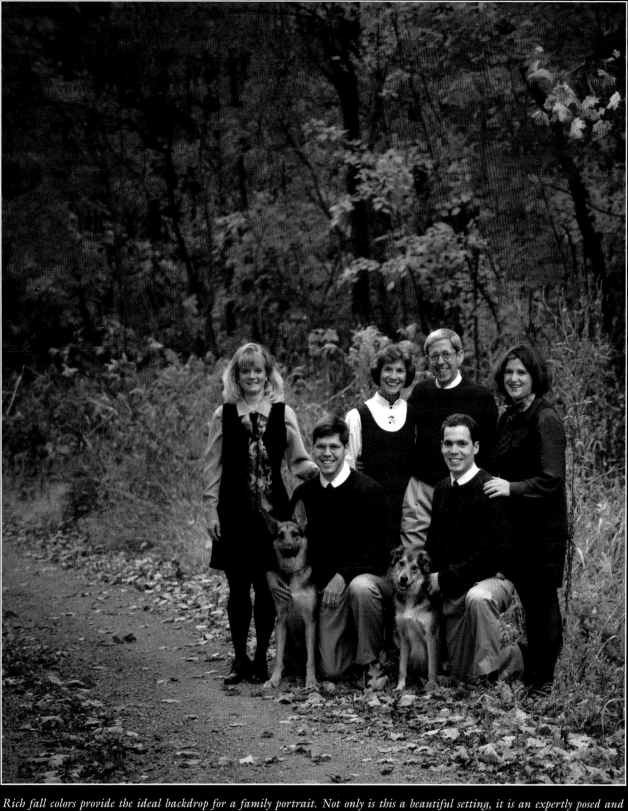

Rich fall colors provide the ideal backdrop for a family portrait. Not only is this a beautiful setting, it is an expertly posed and executed portrait. Note the first phase in understanding how to create a fine group portrait—there is a design to the arrangement of people within the group. Photograph by Michael Ayers.

Robert Love concurs: "Each person in a group must look great—as if they were photographed alone." Love makes it a point, in fact, to pose and create great individual portraits within his groups, a technique that takes time and patience to perfect.

Great group portraits do not only capture everyone in the group looking good; they should have a style and rhythm. Fine group images have direction, motion and all the visual elements that are found in fine portraits and in art. These pictures possess the means to keep a viewer looking and delving long after the visual information in the picture is digested.

In addition to family portraits, you will see many wedding group portraits in this book, primarily because weddings are the occasion for the "spectacular" group, where everyone is dressed formally, looks great and is in a happy and joyous mood. The couple will often require the wedding photographer to shoot a set number of groups from both sides of the family so that there is a permanent and stylized memory of the most important day in their lives.

...small steps are first required before knowledge is attained.

As in any learning process, small steps are first required before knowledge is attained. In this case, I felt it important to include "couples" as groups. The technical and aesthetic problems involved in making a fine portrait of an individual are considerable—adding another person more than doubles the difficulty factor. Also, many of the techniques involved in posing couples are identical to those used in photographing groups of three or more. So couples represent the building blocks of group portraiture. You will find them useful.

It is my hope that you will not only learn the technical side of group portraiture from this book—how to pose, light and photograph groups on a higher plane—but that you will also become a fan of the design systems used in creating compelling group portraits. This is the path to a higher level of photography and self-expression.

To illustrate this book, I have called upon some of the finest and most decorated portrait and wedding photographers in the world. Some of them I know personally, others I know their work well, and many I have heard lecture throughout the country. Some are newcomers to the limelight, but in every case, their group portraits are exemplary. Many of the photographers included in this book have been honored repeatedly by the country's top professional organizations, the Professional Photographers of America (PPA) and Wedding and Portrait Photographers International (WPPI). I want to take the opportunity to thank all of the great photographers for their participation in this book. Without them, this book would not have been possible. I would also like to thank my illustrator and wife, Shell Dominica Nigro, for her enthusiasm and help in preparing this book.

I would especially like to thank the following photographers for their technical assistance and boundless expertise and especially for their endless patience: Michael Ayers, David Bentley, Robert Love, Bill McIntosh, Norman Phillips and Monte Zucker.

While this book will not be the equivalent of years of experience, it is my hope that you will learn from the masters how to photograph groups of people with style, artistry, technical excellence and professionalism.

1

THE TECHNICAL ASPECTS OF
GOOD GROUP PORTRAITURE

A good group portrait is one that flatters each of the subjects and is pleasing to the eye. With a working knowledge of basic portrait techniques, a sense of design and good rapport with your subjects, you can create an image that is both pleasing and salable, and one that each person in the group will cherish.

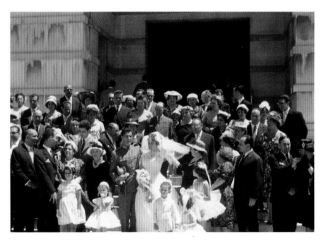

This is not it! It's not a great group portrait. It's not even a decent group snapshot—everyone is looking in different directions. It's the result of someone with a camera at a wedding. It might be minimally valuable fifty years after the big day, but only because it's an historical record. As a group portrait photographer, one must aim considerably higher.

Unlike a fine portrait of an individual, a group portrait conveys a sense of importance and character about the group. A group portrait is most definitely not a snapshot. It has a prearranged sense of design and arrangement of its elements, a uniformity of expression and, in many instances, a coordination of color and clothing. These aspects, of course, are in addition to controlled lighting, posing and composition. So as you may be beginning to see, a fine group portrait is not an easy picture to produce.

The following chapter is an overview of some of the technical aspects of making good exposures for portraiture, and while they may not necessarily be aimed at group portraiture, these techniques are essential to good group portrait photography.

○ CAMERA FORMAT

Large-format cameras and films—4x5 and larger—are certainly good tools with which to make large group portraits. They have inherent camera movements, like swings and tilts, which allow the photographer to "bend" or move the plane of focus to more closely accommodate the shape of the group. Thus, subjects at varying distances from the camera can all be in focus with a few simple camera movements.

The large negative size also makes image quality another of the hallmarks of large format group photography.

However, the biggest limitation of large format is the loss of spontaneity. The photographer must first focus and compose with the lens open on the camera's groundglass. Any corrective swings, tilts or shifts are engaged, the lens is stopped down and then the shutter closed. Once this happens and the photographer inserts a film holder in the camera back, he or she loses contact with the group, at least through the lens. The photographer can no longer see what the lens sees.

The biggest limitation of large format is the loss of spontaneity.

Preparing the camera and subjects for a portrait takes time, even for seasoned photographers. Groups, especially the younger members of the group, quickly lose interest and this will be painfully evident in the proofs. The subjects must remain motionless once the image is focused.

Small and medium format cameras have almost completely replaced large format for group portraiture. There is a wide assortment of lenses and accessories available for these formats. Soft-focus lenses, diffusion and warming filters, a myriad of different focal lengths to choose from and a wide variety of special effects accessories—matte boxes, vignetters and bellows lens shades—are available, making 35mm and medium format the choice of most group portrait photographers.

One of the biggest drawbacks of small format cameras is the inability to retouch the negative. Facial irregularities, such as wrinkles, lines and age spots, cannot be retouched out on a 35mm negative. On medium format negatives, you can do minimal retouching, provided the "head size" is large enough on the negative. However, with groups of three or more, the head size is usually not large enough to retouch on either format.

Most photographers opt for some type of on-camera diffusion, if a softening type of retouching is required. Also, the accessibility of scanners and the wide scope of retouching capabilities found in Adobe® Photoshop® and other image-editing software make negative retouching somewhat less necessary than before. The retouched digital image can either be output directly via an inkjet "photo quality" printer or rewritten to negative film (with the use of a film recorder) so that traditional prints can be made on photographic paper. Retouching a digital image in Photoshop is much less difficult than traditional negative retouching, and the image is "worked" as a positive.

The greatest advantage by far of using small and medium format cameras in group portraiture is the ability to see the subject through the lens just prior to exposure, permitting a much greater range of expressions and poses. Just as important with the smaller formats in group photography is the greater inherent depth of field, meaning that focus is not nearly as critical as it is with large-format, where swings and tilts are often needed merely to hold focus on the group.

○ THE EFFECT OF FOCAL LENGTH

All types of portraiture demand that you use a longer-than-normal lens, particularly for small groups. The general rule of thumb is to use a lens that is 2X the diagonal of the film you are using. For instance, with the 35mm format, a 75 to 85mm lens is a good choice; for the 2¼ inch square format (6x6cm), 100 to 120mm is good, and for 2¼ x 2¾ inch cameras (6x7cm), 110 to 150mm is acceptable.

These optimal portrait lenses, short telephotos, provide normal perspective without subject distortion. If using a "normal" focal length lens (50mm in 35mm format, 75–90mm in the medium formats) you have to move too close to the subject to attain an adequate image size, thereby altering the perspective. This proximity to the subject exaggerates subject features—noses appear elongated, chins jut out, and the backs of heads may appear smaller than normal. The phenomenon is known as foreshortening. The short telephoto provides a greater working distance between camera and subjects while increasing the image size to ensure normal perspective.

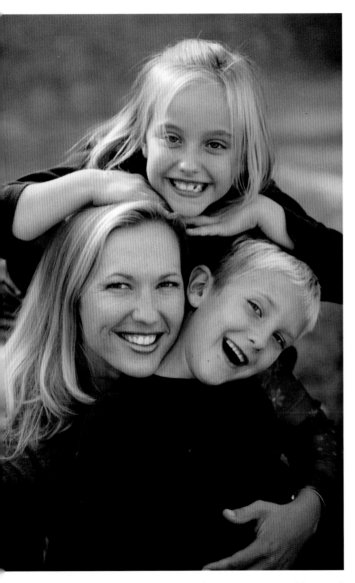

A longer than normal focal length compresses your subjects and separates them from any potentially distracting backgrounds. Notice how completely the background falls out of focus in this charming image. Also note that, while the image seems completely spontaneous, the photographer masterfully positioned all three faces in the same very shallow plane of focus, capturing all three sharply. Photograph by Kenneth Sklute.

Some photographers prefer the longest lens possible when shooting groups because of the aforementioned foreshortening problem; for example, a 150mm lens on a 6x6cm camera. With larger groups, this keeps the people in the back of the group the same relative size as the people in the front of the group.

When space doesn't permit use of a longer lens, shorter lenses must prevail, but observe that the subjects in the front row of a large group may appear much larger than subjects in the back of the group if you get too close.

Wide-angle lenses will actually distort the subjects' appearance, particularly those closest to the frame edges. Raising the camera height, thus placing all subjects at the same relative distance from the lens, can minimize some of this effect.

Conversely, you can use a much longer lens if you have the working room. A 200mm lens, for instance, is a beautiful portrait lens for 35mm because it provides very shallow depth of field and throws the background completely out of focus, providing a backdrop that won't distract from the subjects. When used at wider apertures, this focal length provides a very shallow band of focus that can be used to accentuate just the eyes, for instance, or just the frontal planes of the faces.

Avoid using extreme telephotos (300mm and longer for 35mm). Perspective becomes distorted—subjects' features appear compressed, depending on the working distance—the nose often appearing pasted to the subject's face, and the ears seem parallel to the eyes. Also, you are a far distance away from your subjects with such a lens, making communication difficult or impossible. You want to be close enough so that you can converse normally without shouting out posing instructions.

When making ¾-length or full-length group portraits, it is best to use the normal focal length lens for your camera. This lens will provide normal perspective because you are farther away from your subject than when making a close-up portrait. The only problem you may encounter is that

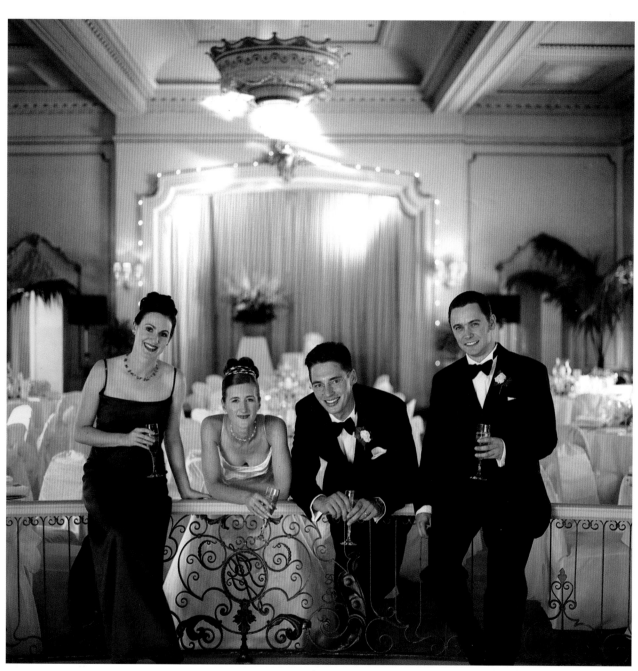

Above: *Working with a slightly longer-than-normal lens and a precisely arranged plane of focus, the photographer was able to shoot at a fairly wide lens aperture in order to throw the background pleasantly out of focus. Sharper image details of the palms and chandelier would have been way too distracting. Photograph by David Anthony Williams.* ***Opposite:*** *Here you see absolutely masterful use of a wide-angle lens for group portraiture. Actually, it's three groups in one portrait. The only wide-angle distortion is visible in the receding squares of the tile floor and the pronounced front chair leg. The photographer turned the background groups inward and kept them away from frame edges, where distortion would be apparent. The wide angle and the wonderful posing produced an intimate storytelling image. Photograph by David Anthony Williams.*

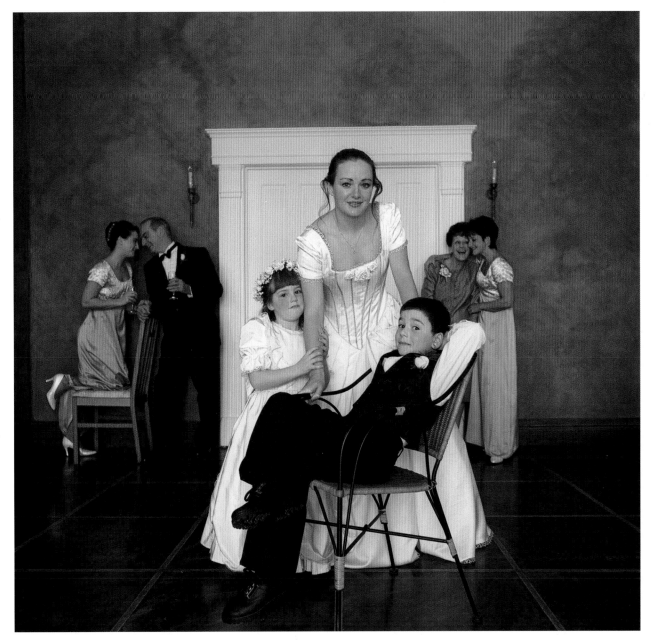

the subjects may not tonally separate from the background with the normal lens. It is desirable to have the background slightly out of focus so that the viewer's attention goes to the subject, rather than to the background. With the normal lens, the depth of field is slightly greater, so that even when working at wide lens apertures, it may be difficult to separate subject from background. This is particularly true when working outdoors, where patches of sunlight or other distracting background elements can easily detract from the subjects.

When making group portraits, you are often forced to use a wide-angle lens. The background problems discussed above can be even more pronounced, but using a wide-angle lens is often the only way you can fit the entire group into the shot and still maintain a decent working distance. For this reason, many expert group photographers carry a stepladder or scope out the location in advance to find a high vantage point, if necessary.

○ LENSES AND DEPTH OF FIELD

Wide-angle lenses have greater inherent depth of field than telephotos. This is why so much attention is paid to focusing telephoto lenses accu-

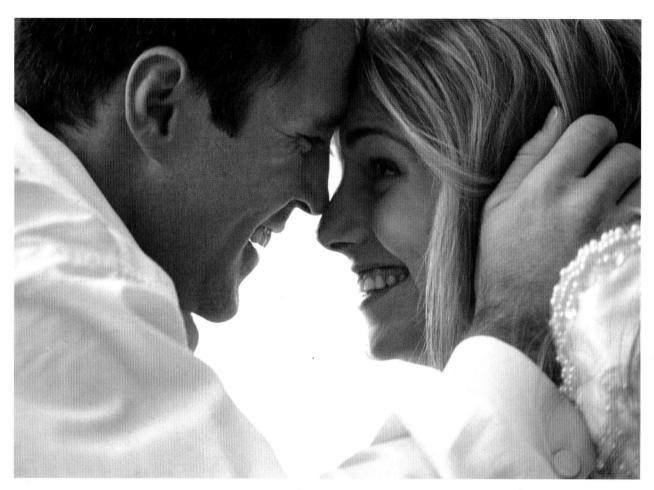

The depth of field needed in a profile portrait is minimal. In this case, the photographer merely had to hold the distance from the tips of the noses to the ears, a distance of only about four inches. Focus falls off at the man's hand and sleeve, without distraction. What has to be sharp is razor sharp. Incidentally, this image was made by using a handheld scrim to diffuse backlighted window light. The image was filled in from the camera side with a reflector. Photograph by Monte Zucker.

rately in portraiture. Also, the closer you are to your subjects, the less depth of field you will have, at any given aperture. When you are shooting a tight image of faces, be sure that you have enough depth of field at your working lens aperture to hold the focus fully on the subjects' faces.

Another thing to remember is that medium-format lenses have less depth of field than 35mm lenses. A 50mm lens on a 35mm camera will yield more depth of field than a 75mm lens on a medium-format camera, even if the lens apertures and subject distances are the same. This is important because many photographers feel that if they go to a larger format, they will improve the quality of their portraits. This is true in that the image will appear improved simply by the increase in film

size; however, focusing becomes much more critical with the larger format.

Learn to use your lens' depth-of-field scale. The viewfinder screen is often too dim when the lens is stopped down with the depth-of-field preview to gauge overall image sharpness accurately. Learn to read the scale quickly and practice measuring distances mentally. Better yet, learn the characteristics of your lenses. You should know what to expect, sharpness- and depth-of-field-wise, at your most frequently used lens apertures, which for most group shots will be f/5.6, f/8 and f/11.

○ DEPTH OF FOCUS

The most difficult type of portrait to focus precisely is a close-up portrait. It is important that the

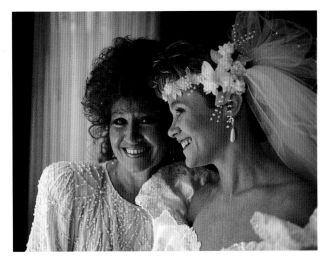

Critical focusing was a must for this image in order to hold both faces in sharp focus. Notice how cleverly the photographer moved to the left to adjust his plane of focus so that a wide lens aperture would accommodate both faces in sharp focus. Photograph by Norman Phillips.

eyes and frontal planes of all the faces in the group be tack-sharp. It is usually desirable for the ears to be sharp as well, but it is not always possible.

When working at wide lens apertures where depth of field is reduced, you must focus carefully to hold the eyes, lips and tip of the nose in focus. This is where a good working knowledge of your lenses is essential. Some lenses will have the majority of their depth of field behind the point of focus; others will have the majority of their depth of field in front of the point of focus. In most cases, the depth of field is split about 50-50—half in front of and half behind the point of focus. It is important that you know how your different focal length lenses operate. It is also important to check the depth of field with the lens stopped down to your taking aperture, using your camera's depth-of-field preview control. As a rule of thumb, with most lenses, if you focus one third of the way into the group or scene, it will ensure optimum depth of focus at all but the widest apertures.

Assuming that your depth of field lies half in front and half behind the point of focus, it is best to focus on the eyes in a group close-up. This will generally keep the faces and the main center of interest, the eyes, in focus. The eyes are a good point to focus on because they are the region of greatest contrast in the face, and thus make focusing easier. This is particularly true for autofocus cameras that often seek areas of highest contrast on which to focus.

Focusing a ¾- or full-length portrait is a little easier because you are farther from the subjects, where depth of field is greater. Again, you should split your focus, halfway between the forwardmost and farthest points that you want sharp on the subject. And again, because of background problems, it is a good idea to work at wide apertures to keep your background moderately soft.

It is also essential for groups of two or more that the faces fall in the same focusing plane. This is accomplished with posing and careful maneuvering of your subjects or your camera position. If one or more of the people in the group is out of focus, the portrait will be flawed.

○ SHIFTING THE FOCUS POINT

Once you have determined the depth of field for a given lens at a given focusing distance and taking aperture (by examining the lens' depth-of-field scale), you now have a range in which you can capture all of your subjects sharply. For example, at a subject-to-film plane distance of 10 feet, an 80mm lens set to f/8 will, hypothetically, produce depth of field stretching from 10 feet to 12 feet, 4 inches, producing an effective depth of field of roughly 28 inches. By shifting the focus point to within that region, you can effectively expand the range of focus to perhaps 36 inches. What does all this mean? It means that in this example you must place all of your subjects within that 28 to 36-inch plane at f/8 for all of your subjects to be sharp.

The above example is critical for photographing groups because you must modify the poses of each person in the group to accommodate that narrow zone of focus; in this example, 28–36 inches. As seen in the diagram on page 16, subjects in the back of the group can lean in and subjects at the front of the group can lean back slightly so that all of your subjects fall within that plane.

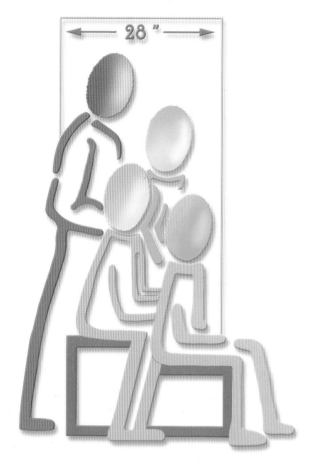

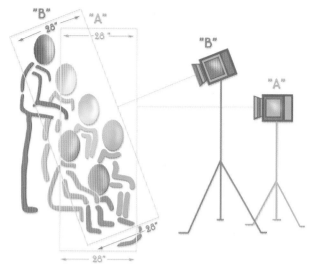

Left: Subjects in the back of the group can lean in and subjects at the front of the group can lean back slightly so that all of your subjects fall within one plane. Above: To include additional subjects in the same amount of space, raise the camera height, angling the camera downward so that the film plane is more parallel to the plane of the group. Diagram concepts courtesy of Norman Phillips.

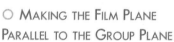

○ MAKING THE FILM PLANE
PARALLEL TO THE GROUP PLANE

Suppose your group is bigger than the one pictured above and you have no more room in which to make the portrait. One solution is to raise the camera height, angling the camera downward so that the film plane is more parallel to the plane of the group. You have not changed the amount of depth of field that exists at that distance and lens aperture, it is still only 28–36 inches, as in the above example, but you have optimized the plane of focus to accommodate that same 28–36-inch range.

○ SHIFTING THE FIELD OF FOCUS

Lenses will characteristically focus objects in a somewhat straight line, but not completely straight. If you line your subjects up in a straight line and back up so that you are roughly 25–30 feet or more from the group, all subjects will be rendered sharply at almost any aperture. The

problem is that at a distance, subjects become unrecognizable, so you must move closer to the group making those at the ends of the group farther away from the lens than those in the middle of the lineup. Those farthest from the lens will be difficult to keep in focus. The solution, simply, is to "bow" the group, making the middle of the group step back and the ends of the group step forward so that all the members of the group are the same relative distance from the camera. To the camera, the group looks like a straight line, but you have actually distorted the plane of sharpness to accommodate the group (see page 18).

Once you begin to see the group portrait in terms of planes of focus, you will soon get the hang of controlling the planes of sharpness. As in the above examples, keeping the film plane parallel to the plane of the group, it is necessary to raise the camera each time another row is added in the back. This also keeps image perspective in check. Otherwise, the people up front appear too large,

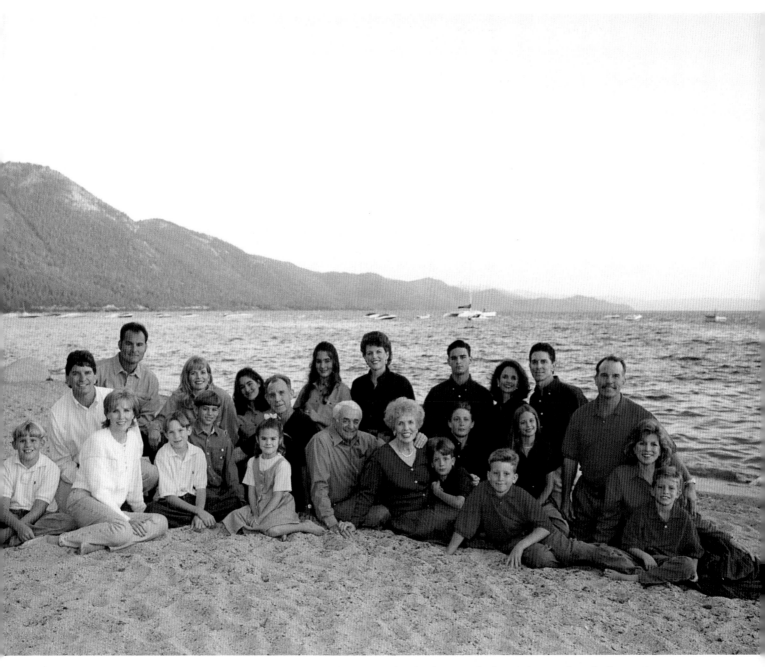

In this large group the photographer shifted the plane of focus by moving those in the center back and those on the ends closer to form a "bow," creating the impression that all subjects are the same relative distance from the camera. This is a technique that helps control your plane of focus when depth of field is at a minimum. Also note that the photographer had each subgroup dress in complementary colors, a technique that will be discussed in chapter 3. Photograph by Robert Love and Suzanne Love.

while the people in the back rows would appear too small.

Another school of thought says to establish one or more subject planes in which to place individuals in the group. These planes will make it simpler for you to finalize your lighting and allow you to include everyone within the camera's range of focus. Sometimes a setting, such as a staircase or a gentle sloping hillside can provide a natural organization of planes.

○ OPTIMUM SHOOTING APERTURES

Choosing the working lens aperture is often a function of exposure level. In other words, you

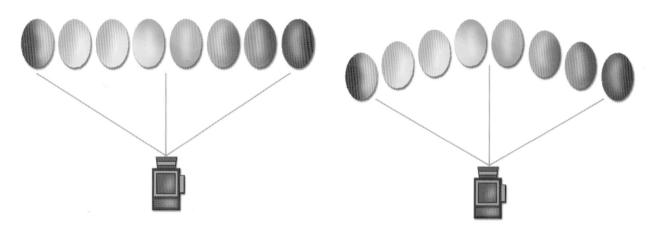

When a straight-line group is configured in front of the camera lens, the subjects directly in front of the lens will be closest to the camera lens. Those at the ends of the group will be a greater distance from the lens. By "bowing" the group (the center-most people taking a step back, the outermost people taking a step forward and everyone in between adjusting) all will be equidistant from the lens, and focus will be a snap—even at wider apertures. Diagram concept courtesy of Norman Phillips.

often don't have much of a choice in the aperture you select, particularly when depth of field for large or deep (front to back) groups is concerned.

Experts in optics design suggest choosing an aperture that is 1½ to 2 full f-stops smaller than the lens' maximum aperture. For instance, the optimum lens aperture of an f/2 lens would be around f/4. Theoretically, this is the sharpest lens aperture the lens offers. Conversely, avoid the minimum lens apertures—f/16 or f/22—because they suffer slight loss of sharpness due to diffraction. Again, this is optimum. More often, the considerations of your group take precedence where aperture selection is concerned.

A lens used wide open (at its maximum aperture) theoretically suffers from spherical aberration; a lens at its smallest apertures suffers from diffraction. Both of these conditions reduce the overall sharpness of the recorded image to a slight degree. Even though at the smaller apertures the lens may produce greater depth of field, the image is still sharpest at or near its optimum aperture—1½ to 2 stops from wide open.

Some photographers choose an aperture that they prefer over all others for groups. Norman Phillips, for instance, prefers f/8 to f/11, even though f/11 affords substantially more depth of field than f/8. He prefers the relationship between the sharply focused subject and the background at f/8, saying that the subjects at f/11 look "chiseled

out of stone." So for Phillips, at least, the optimum aperture is f/8, regardless of lens-sharpness characteristics and depth-of-field considerations.

○ SHUTTER SPEEDS

You should choose a shutter speed that stills both camera and subject movement. If you are using a tripod, $\frac{1}{30}$ to $\frac{1}{60}$ second should be adequate to stop average subject movement. If you are using electronic flash, you are locked into the flash sync speed your camera calls for unless you are "dragging" the shutter (meaning, to work at a slower than flash-sync speed to bring up the level of the ambient light). This effectively creates a balanced flash exposure with the ambient-light exposure.

When working outdoors, you should generally choose a shutter speed faster than $\frac{1}{60}$ second because slight breezes will cause the subjects' hair to flutter, producing motion during the moment of exposure.

If you are handholding the camera, the general rule of thumb is to use the reciprocal of the focal length lens you are using for a shutter speed. For example, if using a 100mm lens, use $\frac{1}{100}$ second (or the next highest equivalent shutter speed, like $\frac{1}{125}$) under average conditions. If you are very close to the subjects, as you might be when making a portrait of a couple, you will need to use a faster shutter speed. When farther away from the sub-

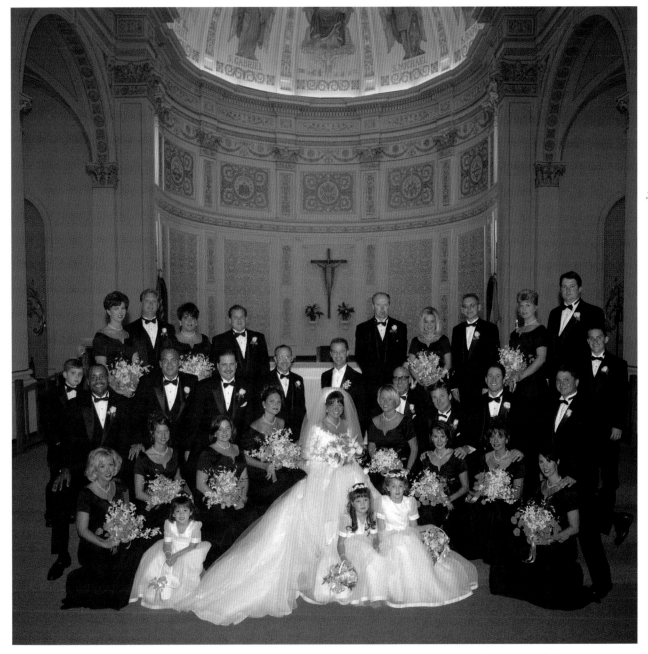

Every time you add a row to the back of the group, the camera height should come up. Notice the bow-tie shape of this very large wedding group. The photographer not only fanned the group up but out, as well. The natural sloping shape of the altar helped him pose the large group. He also dragged the shutter to light the architectural elements of the scene beautifully. Photograph by Michael Ayers.

ject, you can revert to the shutter speed that is the reciprocal of your lens' focal length. Higher image magnification means you need to use a faster shutter speed.

One of the great technical improvements is the development of image stabilization lenses. These lenses optomechanically correct for camera movement and allow you to shoot handheld with long lenses and relatively slow shutter speeds. Canon and Nikon, two companies that currently offer this feature in their lenses, offer a wide variety of zooms and long focal length lenses with image stabilization. If using a zoom, for instance, which has a maximum aperture of f/4, you can still shoot handheld wide open in subdued light at ⅒ or 1/15 of a second and get dramatically sharp results. The

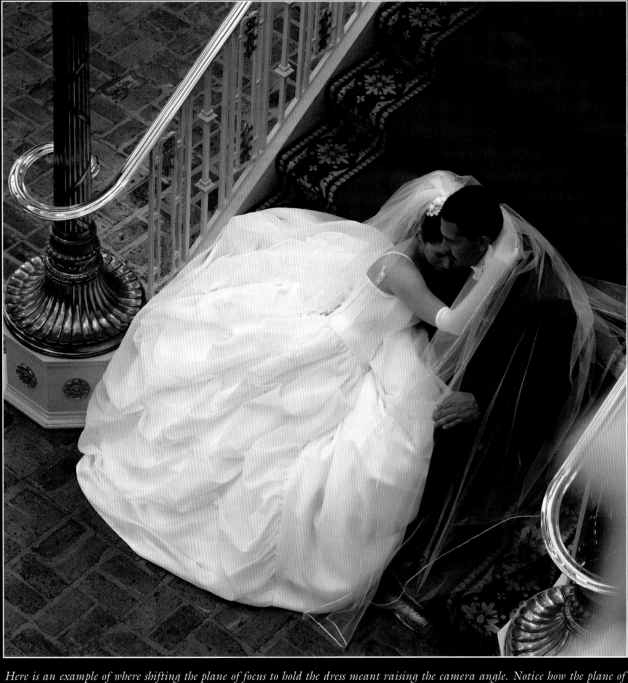

Here is an example of where shifting the plane of focus to hold the dress meant raising the camera angle. Notice how the plane of focus of the subjects is parallel to the camera back, making it relatively simple to hold all of the important elements of the scene in sharp focus. Photograph by Rick Ferro.

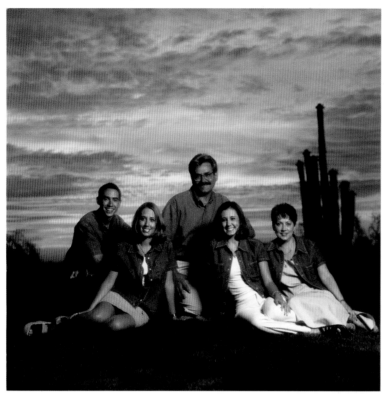

Left: "Dragging the shutter," shooting at a slower shutter speed than the flash-sync speed of the camera, allows you to capture the ambient light in your scene. In this image, the photographer was primarily concerned with the rich desert sky at sunset. The flash output was adjusted to produce the same aperture, but the long shutter speed allowed the sky to be rendered colorfully. Note the position of the diffused flash—above and off-camera by about 45 degrees for the best modeling. Photograph by Kenneth Sklute. *Below:* In this image, the sun had been down five minutes and it was getting dark quickly. The photographer matched the ambient light exposure, $\frac{1}{8}$ second at f/8 with the Lumedyne barebulb strobe at f/8. Camera: Mamiya RZ 67 with 65mm lens, film: Fuji NHG II 800 film. This photographer routinely works at ultraslow shutter speeds like $\frac{1}{4}$ and $\frac{1}{8}$ second. Photograph by Bill McIntosh.

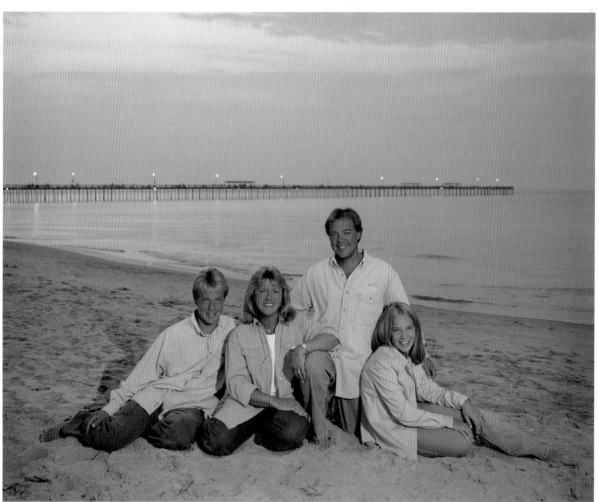

shutter speed and a wider lens aperture. It's more important to freeze subject movement than it is to have great depth of field for this kind of shot. If you have any questions as to which speed to use, always use the next fastest speed to ensure sharper images.

Bill McIntosh, a superb environmental group portrait photographer, will choose shutter speeds that are impossibly long. He works with strobe and often lights various parts of large rooms with multiple strobes. Some of the strobes may be way off in the distance, triggered by radio remotes synced to the shutter release. In order to balance the background strobes with the ambient light in the room and the subject light, he often has to reduce the light on the subject to incorporate all these other elements and consequently ends up shooting at speeds as long as ¼ second. For the inexperienced, shooting groups at these shutter speeds is an invitation to disaster, yet McIntosh routinely does it with incredible results.

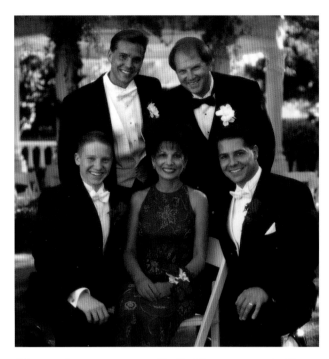

Photographers are creatures of habit. They use a certain film or a family of films because they can predict the films' responses in different situations. Here, the photographer used Kodak Portra 400NC 120 film—part of the Portra film family, which features rich, saturated color, ideal for outdoor group portraits. Photograph by Kenneth Sklute.

○ FILM CHOICE

Extremely slow and extremely fast films should be avoided, generally, for most group situations. Black & white and color films in the ISO 25 range tend to be too contrasty for portraits, and exposure latitude tends to be very slight with these films. With the slower, more contrasty films, you tend to lose delicate shadow and highlight detail if exposure is even slightly off.

Ultrafast films in the ISO 1000 to 3200 range offer an ability to shoot in near darkness but produce a larger-than-normal grain pattern and lower-than-normal contrast. Many photographers use these films in color and black & white for special painterly effects in their images.

Today's color negative films in the ISO 100–400 range have amazing grain structure compared to films of only a few years ago. They often possess mind-boggling exposure latitude, which can range from −2 to +3 stops under or over normal exposure. Optimum exposure is still and will always be recommended, but

to say that these films are forgiving is an understatement.

The two major film companies, Kodak and Fuji, offer "families" of color negative film. Within these families are different speeds, from ISO 160 to 800, for example, and either varying contrast or color saturation. Kodak's Portra films include speeds from ISO 160 to 800 and are available in NC (natural color) or VC (vivid color) versions. Kodak even offers an ISO 100 tungsten-balanced Portra film. Fujicolor Portrait films, available in a similar range of speeds, offer similar skin-tone rendition among the different films as well as good performance under mixed lighting conditions. Once photographers find a family of films they like, they will often stay within that family for all their portrait and wedding photography.

Most medium format and all large format color negative and black & white films have a "tooth," or slightly textured surface, on one side of the film for retouching. This makes retouching leads and dyes adhere to the film surface better. Since 35mm color negative films do not have such a surface, and since the negative is so small, retouching is not recommended with that format, although the film can be "doped" (retouching medium applied) so that it will take dyes and leads if the head size is sufficiently large.

○ BLACK & WHITE FILMS

With black & white portraits, contrast is more important than it is in color portraits, where there is no practical means of altering contrast, except by lighting. You can alter the contrast of a black & white negative by increasing or decreasing development. By increasing negative development, you increase contrast; decrease development and you lower contrast.

This is important to know, because the contrast in your portraits will vary a great deal. Those shot in bright sunlight with a minimum of fill-in illumination, or those shot in other types of contrasty lighting, should be altered in development by decreasing development a minimum of 10 percent. Portraits made under soft, shadowless light, such as umbrella illumination, will have low contrast so the development should be increased at least 10 percent, sometimes even 20 percent. The resulting negatives will be easier to print than if developed normally and will hold much greater detail in the important tonal areas of the portrait.

○ EXPOSURE

In black & white, your goal is to achieve consistent fine-grain negatives with the maximum allowable highlight and shadow detail. If you find that your normally exposed negatives are consistently too contrasty, or not contrasty enough, decrease or increase development accordingly. If your negatives come out consistently over- or underexposed, then you must adjust the film speed you are using to expose the film. For instance, if you use an intermediate-speed ISO film as recommended, and your negatives are consistently

underexposed, lower the ISO (to a setting of 80 or 64, if using ISO 100 or 125 film) to see if that has a beneficial increase in negative density. If your negatives are consistently overexposed, increase the ISO (increase the ISO setting on your meter to ISO 125 or 160, for example).

Film companies are somewhat notorious for overrating the film speed of their products. For that reason, most pros are skeptical and will automatically underrate their film to produce slightly more exposure in the shadows. This is why you see many professionals expose their 400 speed film at an exposure index (E.I.) of 320 and their 800 speed film at E.I. 640. This is true for both color and black & white films.

...know the difference between errors in exposure and errors in development.

It is important to note that before you begin fine-tuning your exposure and development, you should be sure you know the difference between errors in exposure and errors in development. Underexposed negatives lack sufficient shadow detail; underdeveloped negatives lack sufficient contrast. Overexposed negatives lack highlight detail; overdeveloped negatives have excessive contrast but may have sufficient highlight detail. If you are unsure, and most become unsure in the areas of overdevelopment and overexposure, make a test print from the suspect negative. If you cannot obtain highlight detail by printing the negative darker, then the negative is overexposed. If highlight detail appears but only when the negative is printed down, then you have overdeveloped the negative.

○ METERING

Because exposure is so critical to producing fine portraits, it is essential to meter the scene properly. Using an in-camera light meter may not always

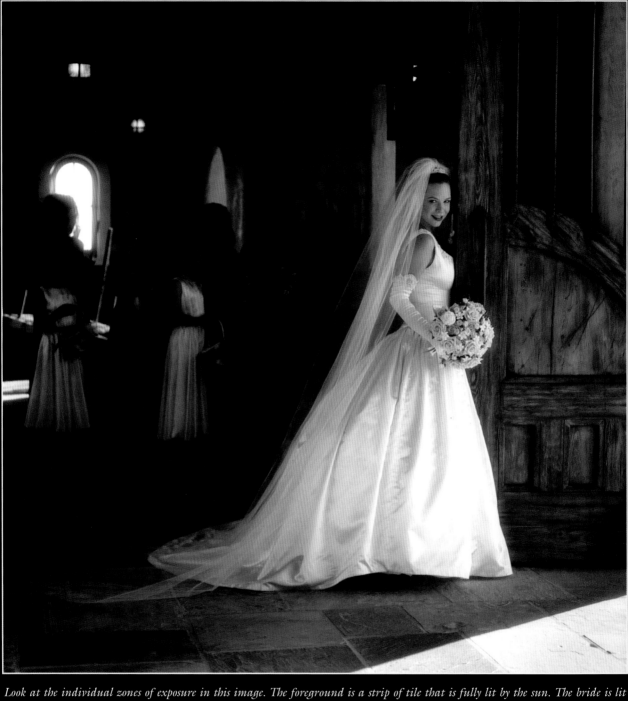

Look at the individual zones of exposure in this image. The foreground is a strip of tile that is fully lit by the sun. The bride is lit indirectly with light bouncing around in the doorway and some diffuse and direct sunlight. The bridesmaids and flower girls are deep in shadow and are just barely visible, an effect this photographer uses on occasion. Knowing the film, its exposure latitude and previsualizing the image made this impossible image a huge success. Photograph by Kenneth Sklute.

give you consistent and accurate results. Even with sophisticated multi-zone in-camera reflectance meters, brightness patterns can influence the all-important skin tones. Usually these meters are center-weighted because that's where most people place their subjects within the frame. The problem arises from the meter's function, which is to average all of the brightness values that it sees to produce a generally acceptable exposure. Put more succinctly, the in-camera meter wants to turn everything it sees into a shade of 18 percent gray. This is rather dark even for well-suntanned or dark-skinned individuals. So, if using the in-camera meter, take a meter reading from an 18 percent gray card held in front of the subjects, large enough to fill most of the frame. If using a handheld reflected-type meter, do the same thing—take a reading from an 18 percent gray card or a surface that approximates 18 percent reflectance.

The preferred type of meter for portraiture is the handheld incident light meter. This does not measure the reflectance of the subjects, but rather measures the amount of light falling on the scene. Simply stand where you want your subjects to be, point the hemisphere (dome) of the meter directly at the camera lens, and take a reading. This type of meter yields extremely consistent results, because it measures the light falling on the subjects rather than the light reflected from the subjects. It is less likely to be influenced by highly reflective or light-absorbing surfaces.

The ultimate meter for groups, especially outdoor groups, is the handheld incident flashmeter, which also reads ambient light. There are a number of models available, but they all allow you to meter both the ambient light at the subject, and the flash output, again, at the subject position. The problem is that you either need to have someone trip the strobe for you, while you hold the meter, or have the subject hold the meter while you trip the strobe to get a reading. You can also attach a PC cord to the meter and trigger the strobe that way, but PC cords can be problematic, particularly when there are children running around. Sooner or later, with weddings and other large groups, somebody is going to trip over the PC cord, pulling the flash, light stand and umbrella down as well.

The solution is to fire the strobe remotely with a wireless triggering device. These devices use transmitters and receivers to send and receive signals to the flash or flashes that are part of the system. There are several types of wireless triggering devices. Optical slaves work with bursts of light, such as that from a single electronic flash. The other lights, equipped with optical receivers, sense the pulse of flash light and fire at literally the same instant.

The solution is to fire the strobe remotely with a wireless triggering device.

Radio slaves send radio signals in either analog or digital form. Digital systems can be used almost anywhere and they aren't adversely affected by nearby radio transmissions. For a completely wireless setup you can use a separate wireless transmitter for the handheld light meter. This allows you the ultimate in cordless metering, since you can meter the ambient and flash exposures from the subject position without the need of an assistant or PC cord. The unit fires the flash or multiple flashes wirelessly, in a similar manner to the transmitter on the camera.

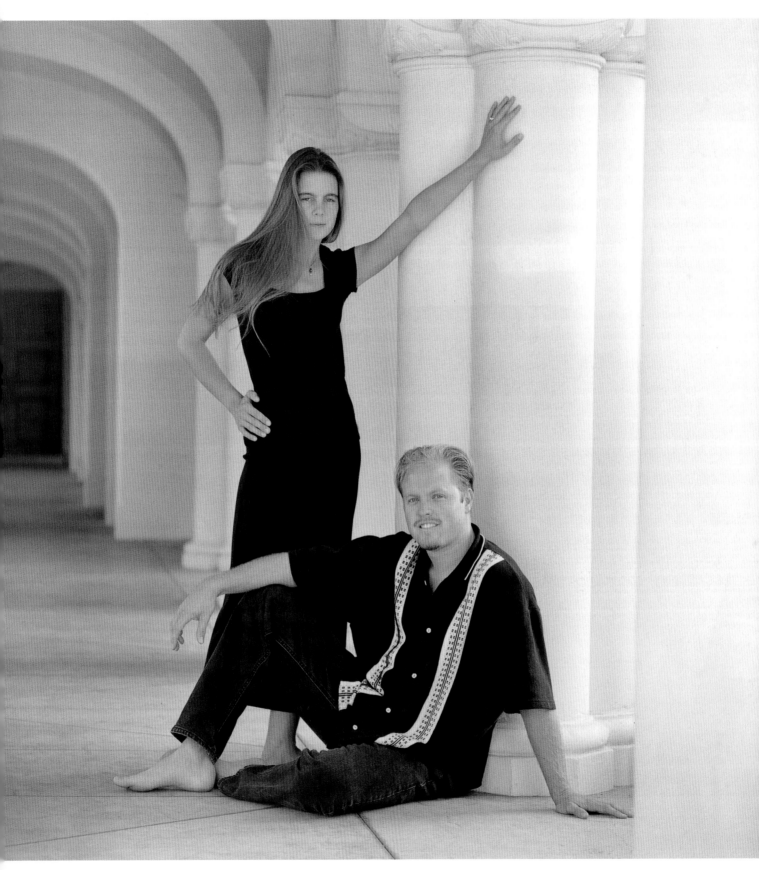

This is a masterful rendering of delicate tones, which could only be preserved by precise exposure. The photographer previsualized how the columns in the foreground should be lighter than those in the receding hallway, by using fill-flash, which would also lower the lighting ratio on the faces. She held the difficult dark tones of the clothing and the delicate specular highlights in the faces. Photograph by Heidi Mauracher.

$\left(2\right)$

POSING AND COMPOSITION

When more than one person is pictured in a portrait, the traditional rules of portraiture, dating back to Greek civilization and refined throughout the centuries, have to be bent, if not shattered completely. As one noted portrait photographer, Norman Phillips, says, "the most important concern in building groups is to be sure they are in focus and properly lighted."

In traditional portraiture of a single person, the fundamental posing and composition help define character in the image. In a group portrait it is the design created by more than one person that helps to define the image. As you will see, there are a number of tricks at play that you probably have never noticed.

○ SUBJECT POSITIONING
When "designing" groups, which may take some time, it is important that your subjects appear to feel comfortable. This is particularly true for large groups. Posing stools and benches allow the subject comfort, and also provide good, upright posture. These are fine for studio work, but what about outdoors or on location? You must find a spot—a hillside or an outdoor chair, for example—that will be relatively comfortable for

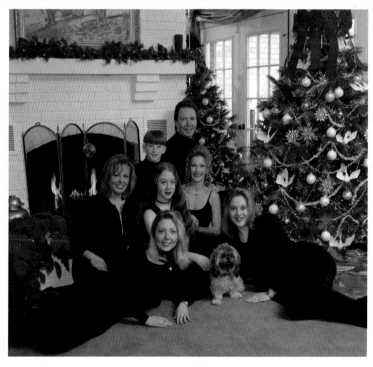

Here's what's important in a good group portrait: Everyone in the group must look great! Here, everyone and everything in the photograph looks great, from the dog to the Christmas tree. Notice too that the photographer created the timeless pyramid pattern for this group composition. Ceiling bounce flash was used to make the image, and the photographer matched the indoor flash exposure to the outdoor daylight exposure so detail would be visible outside. Photograph by Michael Ayers.

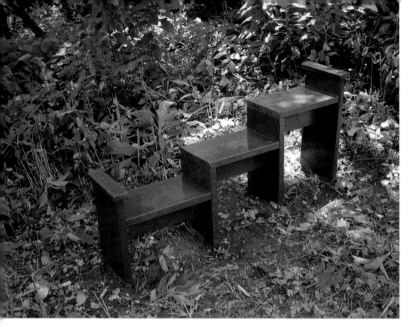

the duration of the shooting session. This will help your posing to appear natural.

Poses should feel natural to the subject. If your subjects are to appear relaxed, then the poses must be not only natural to them, but typical.

○ HEAD AND SHOULDERS AXIS

One of the fundamentals of good portraiture is that the subjects' shoulders should be turned at an angle to the camera. When the shoulders face the camera straight on, it makes people look wider than they really are and it can lead to a static composition.

Not only should the shoulders be at an angle, so should each subject's head. This is known as the head and shoulders axis, each having a different plane and angle. Technically speaking, these are imaginary lines running through shoulders (shoulder axis) and down the ridge of the nose (head axis). Head and shoulder axes should never be perpendicular to the line of the lens axis.

With men, the head is more often turned the same direction as the shoulders, but not necessarily to the same degree. With women, the head is often at a slightly different and opposing angle.

*Top: One of the basic techniques of group portraiture is to position your subjects at different levels to produce dynamic lines within the composition. A posing bench, such as this homemade one by photographer Michael Ayers, is ideal for outdoor posing where people often don't want to be posed directly on the ground. It seats five—one on each seat and one on each armrest. Six more can stand behind the bench with more seated in front. Photograph by Michael Ayers. **Bottom:** This very unusual wedding portrait illustrates the mental image that bride and groom might have of one another—an imagined portrait, if you will. The image also illustrates the concept of head and shoulder axis, where the shoulders are turned one direction, while the head is turned at a slightly different angle. The groom is posed with his head turned at a similar angle as his shoulders —as is the bride—but in both cases, the angles are slightly different. Head and shoulder axis is something you should be conscious of, regardless of whether you follow the guidelines rigorously or not. Photograph by Vladimir Bekker.*

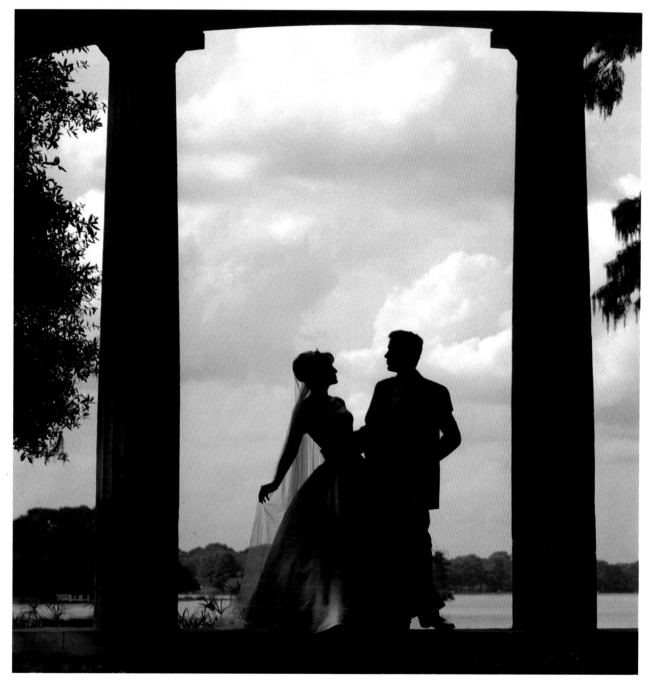

Silhouetted profiles can reveal as much about the character of your subjects as a frontal view. Note that in this image both the bride and groom's shoulders are turned at a different angle than their heads. Both have chins tilted up, the groom has a slight space in the crook of his elbow and there is a very slight space between the two subjects so that their forms do not merge. There's a touch of elegance in this image—notice the pose of the bride's hand as she delicately holds her veil away from her dress. Powerful, silhouetted columns, heightening the perceived importance of the event, frame and balance the couple. Photograph by Rick Ferro.

One of the byproducts of good posing is the introduction of dynamic lines into the composition. The line of the shoulders now forms a diagonal line, while the line of the head creates a different dynamic line.

○ HEAD POSITIONS

⅞ View. There are three basic head positions in portraiture. The ⅞ view is created when the subject is looking slightly away from the camera. If you consider the full face as a head-on type of

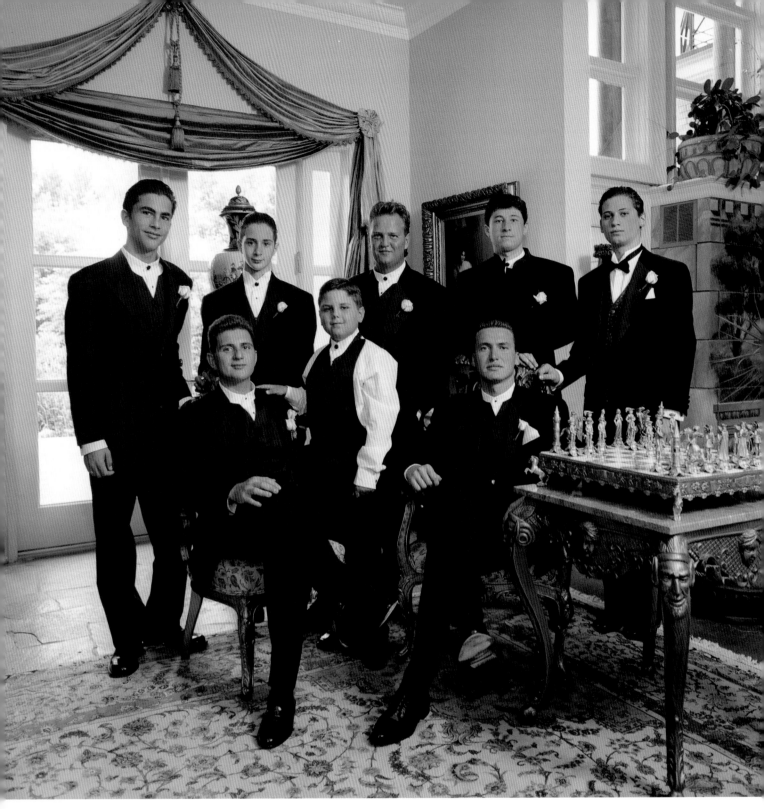

This portrait illustrates many excellent posing points, including showing a variety of head positions. You can see the ⅞ and ¾ facial views, as well as the head-on view, which isn't recommended but is sometimes inevitable in a group this size. Also, notice how well hands—and particularly the feet—are posed. Without looking odd, the seated subjects' feet are not pointing directly into the camera (a posing no-no). Legs are crossed with style and the entire portrait comes across as elegant and upscale, with each member of the group looking important. The only exception is the man on the far left, whose feet are posed too close together. Photograph by Vladimir Bekker.

"mug shot," then the ⅞ view is when the subject's face is turned just slightly away from the camera. In other words, you will see a little more of one side of the face. You will still see the subject's far ear in a ⅞ view.

¾ View. This is when the far ear is hidden from the camera and more of one side of the face is visible. With this pose, the far eye will appear smaller because it is farther away from the camera than the near eye. It is important when posing subjects in a ¾ view to position them so that the smallest eye (people usually have one eye that is slightly smaller than the other) is closest to the camera. This way both eyes appear, perspective-wise, the same size in the photograph.

Profiles. In the profile, the head is turned almost 90 degrees to the camera. Only one eye is visible. In posing your subjects in a profile position, have them turn their heads gradually away from the camera position just until the far eye and eyelashes disappear from view. If the subject has exceptionally long eyelashes, they will still show up, even when the head is turned 90 degrees or more.

In the profile, the head is turned almost 90 degrees to the camera.

With all three of these head poses, the shoulders should be at an angle to the camera.

Knowing the different head positions will help you provide variety and flow to your group designs. You may, at times, end up using all three head positions in a single group portrait. The more people in the group, the more likely that becomes.

○ TILTING THE HEAD
Each subject's head should be tilted at a slight angle in literally every portrait. By doing this, you slant the natural line of the person's eyes. When the face is not tilted, the implied line is straight and parallel to the bottom edge of the photograph, leading to a repetitive line. By tilting the person's face right or left, the implied line becomes diagonal, making the pose more dynamic.

In men's portraits (this is controversial and not without its detractors), the rule is to tilt the head toward the far shoulder (the one farthest from the camera). In women's portraits, the head should be tipped toward the near shoulder for a supposedly feminine look. These rules are frequently broken, because individual subject characteristics and lighting usually determine whether the person looks masculine or feminine.

For the most natural look, the tilt of the person's head should be slight and not overly exaggerated.

○ HEAD LEVELS AND PLACEMENT IN GROUPS
No two heads should ever be on the same level when next to each other, or directly on top of each other. This is only done in team photos as a rule. Not only should heads be on different levels, but subjects should be as well. In a group of five people you can have all five on a different level—for example: one seated, one standing to the left or right, one seated on the arm of the chair, one kneeling on the other side of the chair, one kneeling down in front with their weight on their calves. Always think in terms of multiple levels. This makes any group portrait more pleasing.

Monte Zucker, who composes very tight, intimate group portraits, has a slightly different take: "I try to never put two heads together at the same level, unless there's another person between them or above or below them."

Regarding proximity of one head to another, be consistent. Don't have two heads close together and two far apart. There should be equal distance between each of the heads. If you have a situation where one person is seated, one standing and a third seated on the arm of the chair (placing the two seated heads in close proximity), then back up and make the portrait a full-length. This minimizes the effect of the standing subject's head being so far from the others.

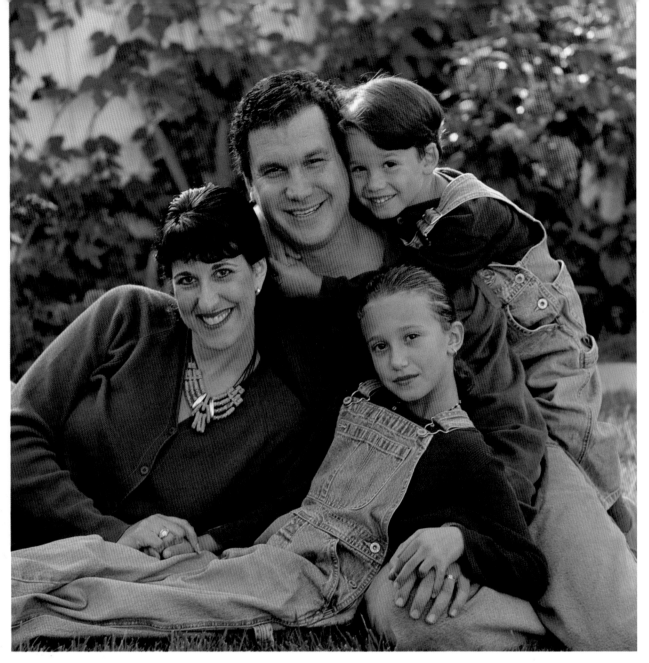

There is more to the posing rule, "no two heads should be on the same level" than simply adjusting the head heights of your subjects so that all are different. The placement of faces should form a pleasing pattern that provides visual direction and keeps the viewer's eye wandering through the image. The photographer created a beautiful flowing diagonal line that follows mom's right arm up through the topmost faces and down to sister's face, where another sweeping diagonal line takes you down to mom's hands, where the visual voyage starts again. Very subtle design is at work here, but it is one reason this portrait is so compelling. Another reason for this photo's success is the close physical connection between family members. Photograph by Heidi Mauracher.

○ THE EYES AND COMMUNICATION

The best way to keep your subjects' eyes active and alive is to engage them in conversation. Look up often while you are setting up and try to find a common frame of interest. Ask questions that might interest any or all members of the group. If the group is uncomfortable or nervous, you have to intensify your efforts to help them get relaxed and comfortable. It's all about trust. If they trust that you know what you're doing and you're a professional, your job will be easy. Try a variety of conversational topics until you find one they warm up to and then pursue it. As you gain their interest, you will take their minds off of the session.

The direction in which the group is looking is important. Start the portrait session by having the group look at you. Using a cable release with the camera tripod-mounted forces you to become a "host" and allows you to physically hold the group's attention. It is a good idea to shoot a few shots of the group looking directly into the camera, but most people will appreciate some variety. Looking into the lens for too long will bore your subjects.

One of the best ways to enliven a group's eyes is to tell an amusing story. If they enjoy it, their eyes will smile. This is one of the most endearing expressions a human being can make.

When photographing groups of any size, you will undoubtedly get some "blinkers." Be on the lookout and if you suspect one of the group blinked during the exposure, they probably did. This problem gets worse as the group gets bigger.

Also crucial in tightly packed groups is the ability of the camera to see the entire face of each subject. This is especially true with kids who will hide behind their mom or big sister so the camera can only see one eye. The best tip is to tell the group "Make sure you can see the camera with both eyes." If they can, you'll get full faces in your groups.

Top: The eyes are the focal point of this lovely portrait. The photographer created a dynamic by letting the diagonal line of the eyes dictate the flow and cropping of the image. Notice too that the eyes of the subjects are engaged and lively, as if the photographer just told them something amusing. Photograph by David Anthony Williams. **Bottom:** *The bigger the group, the more difficult it is to animate all the members at the same time. This is compounded when there are children in the portrait, since what amuses kids might not amuse adults. Notice the lack of tension in all four smiles. All are relaxed and look fantastic. A strong diagonal forms the base of the portrait and the family is decidedly color coordinated, a trademark of this photographer. Photograph by Bill McIntosh.*

○ MOUTHS AND EXPRESSIONS . . . AND COMMUNICATION

It is a good idea to shoot a variety of portraits, some smiling, some serious—or at least not smiling. People are self-conscious about their teeth and mouths. If you see that your group has attractive smiles, make plenty of exposures.

One of the best ways to create natural smiles is to praise your subjects. Tell them how good they look and how much you like a certain feature of

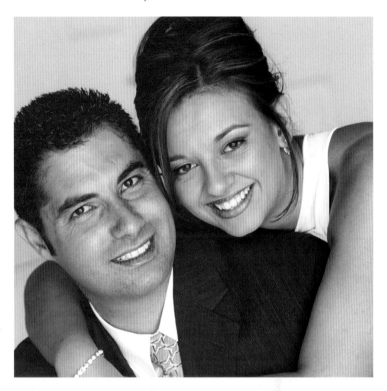

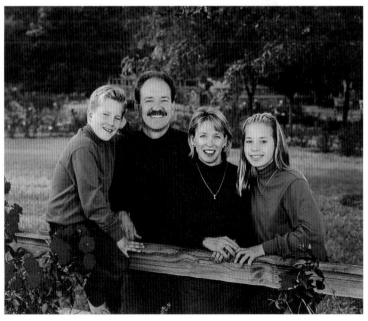

theirs. Simply to say "smile" will produce that life-less, "say cheese" type of portrait. By sincere confidence-building and flattery you will get the group to smile naturally and sincerely and their eyes will be engaged.

The mouth is nearly as expressive as the eyes. Pay close attention to your subjects' mouths to be sure there is no tension; this will give the portrait an unnatural, posed look. If you spot someone in the group that needs relaxing, talk to him or her directly, in a calm, positive manner. An air of re-laxation relieves tension, so work to achieve that mood.

An area of the face where problems occasional-ly arise is the frontal-most part of the cheeks—the part of the face that wrinkles when a person smiles. These are called laugh lines. Some people have very deep furrows that look unnaturally deep when they are photographed smiling. If the lines are severe, avoid a "big smile" type of pose.

○ CHIN HEIGHT
Be aware of the effects of too high or too low a chin height. If the chin is too high, the pose is "snooty." If the chin height is too low, the neck will look compressed, or worse, like the person has no neck at all. A medium chin height is, quite obviously, recommended.

○ CAMERA HEIGHT AND PERSPECTIVE
When photographing groups, there are a few gen-eral rules that govern camera height in relation to the subjects. These rules will produce normal perspective.

For small groups being photographed close-up, the rule of thumb is that camera height should be parallel to the middle face in the grouping. For ¾-length portraits, the camera should be at a height approximately midway between the waists and necks of the subjects. In full-length portraits, the camera should be at around chest height of the tallest subject.

In each case, the camera is at a height that divides the subjects into two equal halves in the

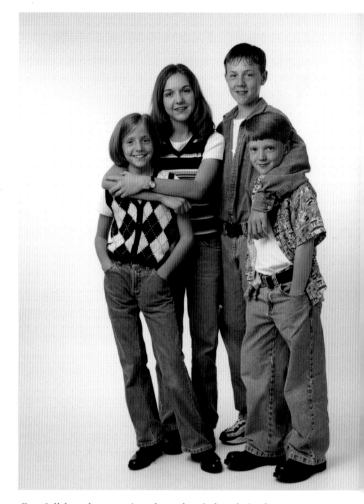

For full-length portraits, the rule of thumb is that camera height should be at roughly the chest height of the tallest member of the group, which it is. Notice too the great "kid" posing, wherein all are in relaxed, natural poses. The affection these sib-lings have for one another is heightened by all of them being con-nected and touching in the portrait. Photograph by J. J. Allen.

viewfinder. This is so that the features above and below the lens/subject axis are the same distance from the lens, and thus recede equally for "nor-mal" perspective. As you will see, when the cam-era is raised or lowered, the perspective (the size relationship between parts of the photo) changes. Raise the camera and feet get smaller. Lower the camera and heads get smaller. By controlling per-spective, you will not only render your subjects more faithfully, you will instill a visual logic into the pic-ture that the viewer finds subliminally reassuring.

○ POSING HANDS

Hands can be a problem in small groups. Despite their small size, they attract attention to themselves, particularly against dark clothing. They can be especially problematic in seated groups, where at first glance you might think there are more hands than there should be. A general rule of thumb is to either show all of the hand or none of it. Don't allow a thumb or half a hand or a few fingers to show. Hide as many hands as you can behind flowers, hats or other people. Be aware of these potentially distracting elements and look for them as part of your visual inspection of the frame before you make the exposure. Award-winning wedding photographer Kenneth Sklute makes it a point to eliminate as many hands as possible in his group portraits. For men, have them put their hands in their pockets. For women, try to hide their hands in their laps or behind other people in the group.

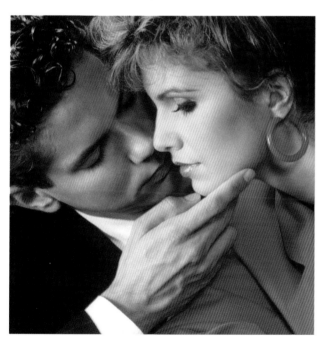

Monte Zucker is a master of posing hands. Here, he breaks a rule and photographs the back of the groom's hand. But the delicate line it produces leads your eye to the bride's eyes, a fundamental necessity when using line to design a group or couples' portrait. Note that by placing lips close together without touching, the photographer created a very romantic portrait. Photograph by Monte Zucker.

The smaller the group, the more likely you will need to pose the hands. So here are a few generalizations about posing hands. One basic rule is never to photograph a subject's hands pointing straight into the camera lens. This distorts the size and shape of the hands. Always have the hands at an angle to the lens.

Photograph the outer edge of the hand, when possible. This gives a natural, flowing line to the photograph and eliminates the distortion that occurs when the hand is photographed from the top or head-on.

Try to "break" the wrist, meaning to raise the wrist slightly so there is a smooth bend and gently curving line where the wrist and hand join. This is particularly important with women whose hands are small. The "break" in the wrist gives the hand dimension.

Photograph the fingers with a slight separation in between. This gives the fingers form and definition. When the fingers are closed tightly together, they appear two-dimensional.

It is important that the hands of a woman have grace, and the hands of a man have strength.

When some of your subjects are standing, hands become a real problem. If you are photographing a man, folding the arms across his chest is a good strong pose. Remember, however, to have the man turn his hands slightly inward, so the edge of the hand is more prominent than the top of the hand. In such a pose, have him lightly grasp his biceps, but not too hard or it will look like he's cold. Also, remember to instruct the man to bring his folded arms out from his body a little bit. This slims down the arms, which would otherwise be flattened against his body, making them and him appear larger. Separate fingers slightly.

With a standing woman, one hand on a hip and the other at her side is a good standard pose. Don't let the free hand dangle. Instead, have her twist the hand so that the outer edge shows to the camera. Always create a break in the wrist for a more dynamic line.

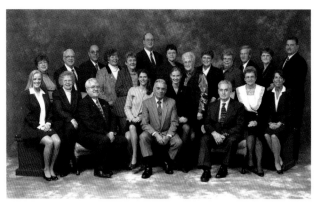

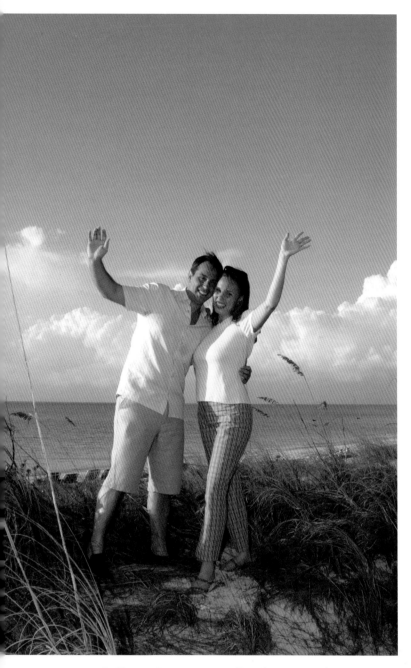

*Left: Monte really doesn't know how to pose hands badly. Even in this beach portrait reminiscent of a '40s film ad, notice how the woman's right hand is hidden, while the man's left hand is clearly visible on her back. And notice the break of the wrists in the waving hands—a masculine and a feminine version of how to treat hands. Photograph by Monte Zucker. **Above:** In this large and ambitious group portrait, there are a number of seated women, some with legs crossed, some not. The closest to correct posing is the woman on the far right, who has her ankles crossed, but with the back leg behind the front leg. Technically, it should be the other way around. You can get a good idea of possible poses of seated women by analyzing this photo. The young woman in the middle has her front leg tucked in behind her back leg for an effective pose. No one's legs are pointing straight into the lens, a conscious effort on the part of the photographer. Photograph by Michael Ayers.*

○ THREE-QUARTER AND FULL-LENGTH POSES

As you probably understand by now, the more of the human anatomy you include in a portrait, the more problems you encounter. When you photograph a group in a ¾- or full-length pose, you have arms, legs, feet and the total image of the body to contend with.

A ¾-length portrait is one that shows the subjects from the head down to a region below the waist. Usually a ¾-length portrait is best composed by having the bottom of the picture

be mid-thigh or below the knee and above the ankles. Never break the portrait at a joint, as this has a negative (though subconscious) psychological impact.

Always have the subjects facing one direction or another, usually at a 30- to 45-degree angle to the camera.

Always have subjects put their weight on their back feet, rather than distributing their weight evenly on both feet or worse yet, on their front foot. There should be a slight bend in the front knee if a person is standing. This helps break up the static line of a straight leg. The back leg can remain straightened.

Have the feet pointing at an angle to the camera. Just as it is undesirable to have the hands facing the lens head-on, so it is with the feet, but

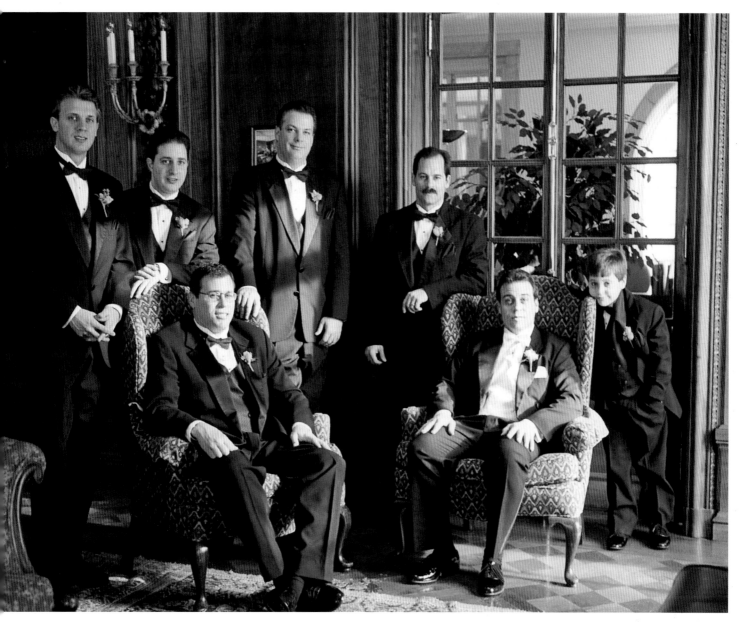

Posing a medium-sized group can be difficult, but when you start taking a pose apart, if certain basics are well performed, it will be a successful image. The group is formed around the two seated men. Notice the well posed hands and how each member of the group is in a relaxed, yet unique pose. Legs are crossed well for men (front ankle crossed over back) and there are dynamic lines flowing throughout the composition. Photograph by Norman Phillips.

even more so. Feet tend to look stumpy and very unattractive when photographed head-on.

When subjects are sitting, a cross-legged pose is desirable. Have the top leg facing at an angle and not into the camera lens. With a woman who is sitting cross-legged, it is a particularly good idea to have her tuck the calf of the front leg in behind the back leg. This reduces the size of the calves, since the back leg, which is farther from the cam-

era, becomes the most important visually. Always have a slight space between the leg and the chair, when possible, as this will slim thighs and calves. And don't allow seated subjects to sit back in the chair with their lower back in contact with the chair back. This thickens the person, especially in the torso.

The subjects' arms should never be allowed to fall to their sides, but should project outward to

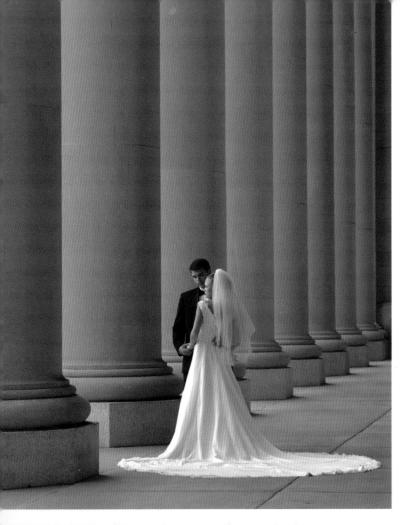

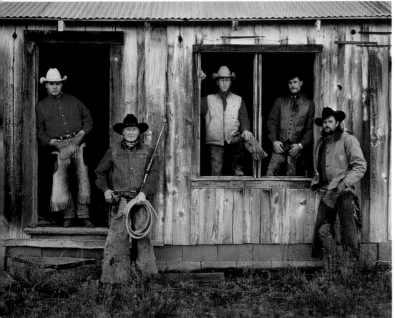

triangular base in the composition visually attracts the viewer's eye upward, toward the subjects' face. This little trick of keeping the arms apart from the torso also helps the arms look well defined and slender, which is particularly important to women.

As you will see, the seated pose is often the cornerstone of the small group. A mother or grandmother is often the seated one and the center of the group, around which the rest of the group is designed.

It should be noted that in any discussion of subject posing, the two most important points are that the poses appear natural (one that the people would typically fall into), and that the subjects' features be undistorted. If the pose is natural and the features look normal, perspective-wise, then you have achieved your goal, and the portrait will be pleasing to you and the subject.

○ COMPOSITION

Composition for groups is much different than composition for individual portraits. The rules remain the same, but the difference is that a member or several members of the group become the primary areas of interest. For example, the grand-

provide gently sloping lines, which form a "base" to the composition. This is achieved by asking the subjects to separate their arms from their torsos; have them be aware that there should be a slight space between their upper arms and torsos. This

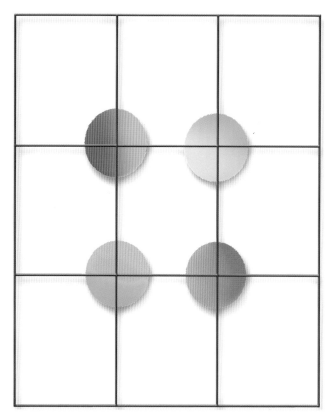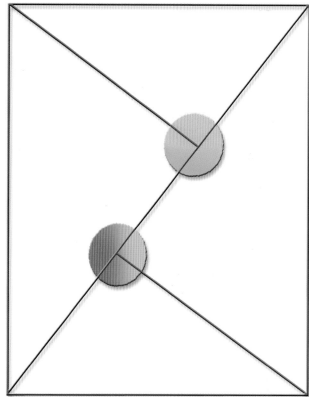

The rule of thirds (left) and the golden mean (right) are two ways of achieving dynamic compositions in group portrait photography. In each case, the center of interest should be placed on or near an intersection of two lines within the picture rectangle. Examine the portraits in this chapter and see if you can find the intersections within the frame where the centers of interest lie.

parents in a family portrait, or the bride and groom in a wedding group are the main centers of interest and as such, should occupy a prime location within the composition.

○ THE RULE OF THIRDS

One of the basics in image composition is the rule of thirds. The rectangular viewing area is cut into nine separate squares by four lines. Where any two lines intersect is an area of dynamic visual interest. The intersecting points are ideal spots to position the main subjects in the group.

The main point of interest does not necessarily have to fall at an intersection of two lines. It could also be placed anywhere along one of the dividing lines.

In close-up groups, the eyes are the areas of central interest. Therefore, it's wise to position the subjects on a dividing line or at an intersection of two lines.

In a ¾- or full-length portrait, the faces are the centers of interest, thus the primary subject's face should be positioned to fall on an intersection or on a dividing line. This is significant, because if it is a portrait of a bride and groom, the bride should be configured prominently.

In doing environmental portraiture, where the surroundings play a big part in the design of the image, the rule of thirds is crucial to use for primary and secondary points of interest.

○ THE GOLDEN MEAN

The golden mean represents the point where the main center of interest should lie and it is an ideal compositional type for portraits, individual or groups. The golden mean is found by drawing a diagonal from one corner of the frame to the other. A second line is then drawn from one or both of the remaining corners so that it intersects the first line perpendicularly. By doing this you can

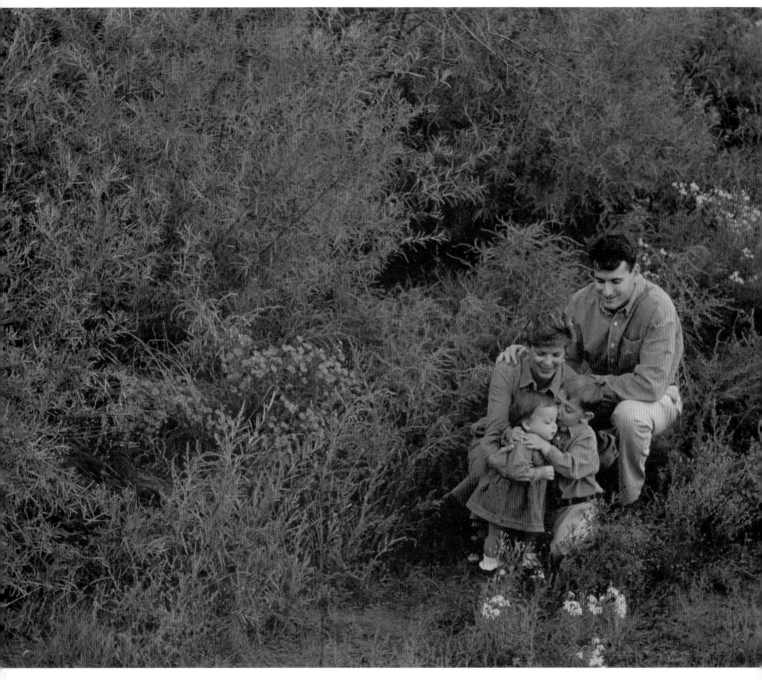

This delightful family portrait was made very late in the day. The path they're on is barely visible, yet the line of the path, outlined in yellow flowers, helps define a diagonal third of the image. The group, who are all touching and connected, forms a single unit to the eye and is perceived as a group and not four individuals. A secondary point of interest is the bouquet of purple asters on the left. Both centers of interest fall on intersecting lines in a rule of thirds grid. Hasselblad with 80mm lens, Fuji MPN film exposed for $\frac{1}{30}$ at f/8. Photograph by Frank Frost.

The design of this engagement couple's portrait is flawless. The stand of trees in the upper left occupies one of the intersections of the rule of thirds. The line of the white rocks meanders up and through the image in a flowing diagonal, as does the stream. Natural backlight with no fill was used along with a Mamiya RB 67 with 65mm lens. By choosing a high vantage point, the photographer eliminated distracting sky and background elements, making the subjects more prominent in the image. Photograph by Bill Duncan.

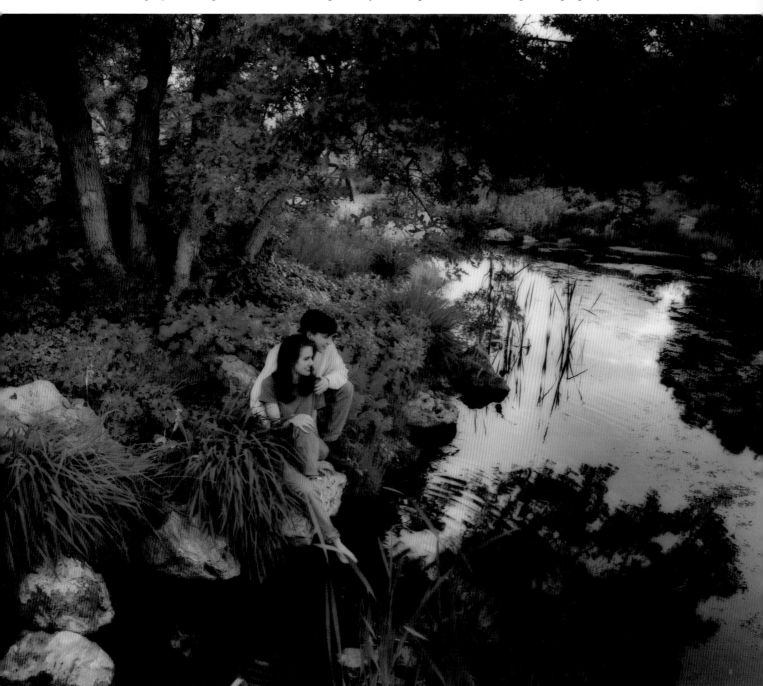

determine the proportions of the golden mean for either horizontal or vertical photographs. It should be noted that if the group is facing right, then you should position them on the left side of the frame. If facing left, the group should be positioned on the right. This provides the necessary direction in the portrait.

○ DIRECTION

Regardless of which direction the subjects are facing in the photograph, there should be slightly more room in front of the group on the side toward which they are facing. For instance, if the group is looking to the right as you look at the scene through the viewfinder, then there should

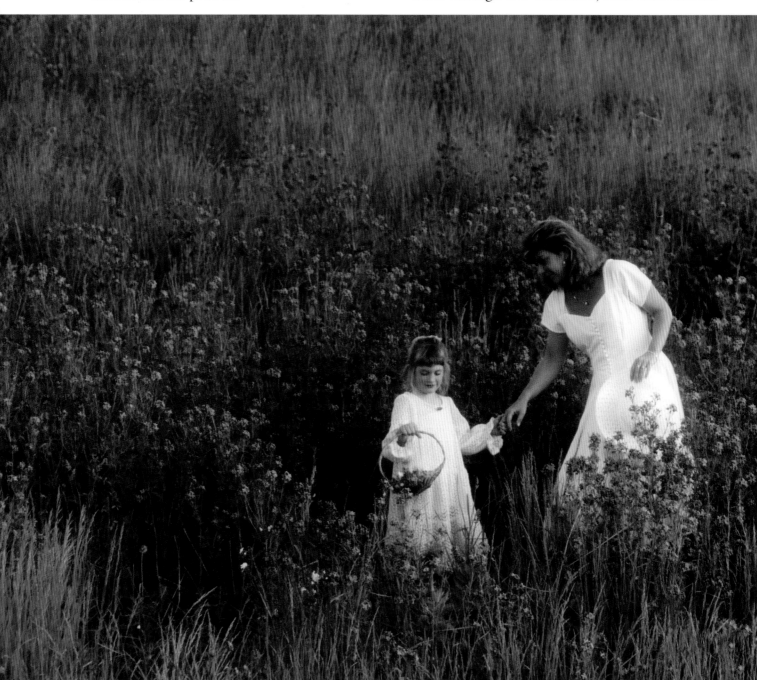

In this very soft and beautiful portrait of mother and child, not only is the placement of the subjects perfectly balanced on the golden mean but there is great direction in the print. The purple flowers flow around the subjects, embracing them. And in the tall grass, you can see the traces of other curving trail lines above and below the group. All of these elements serve to enhance an already fine portrait. Photograph by Gary Fagan.

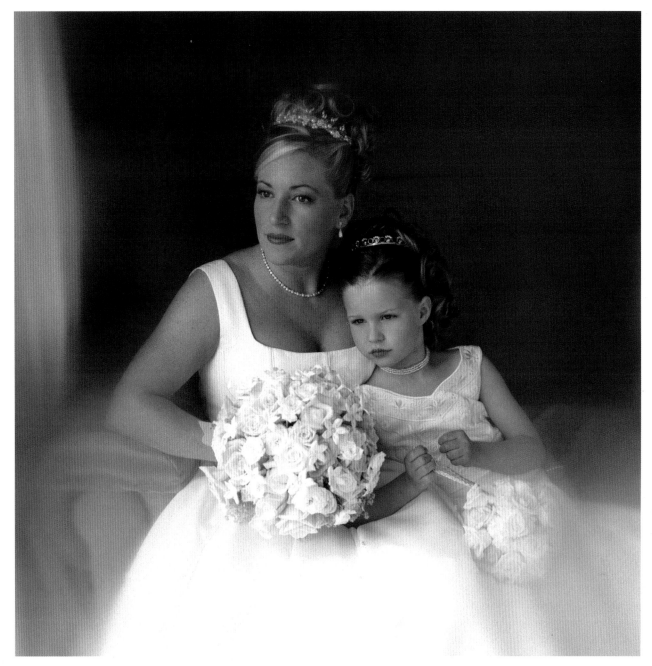

Look at the elegant shapes found in this portrait. The elbows of the bride and little girl form a graceful pyramid. The wedding dress forms a secondary pyramid and acts as a horizontal base for the portrait. Both shapes are compelling and the image is topped off with priceless expressions and timeless window lighting. Photograph by Anthony Cava.

be more space to the right side of the subject than to the left of the group in the frame. This gives a visual sense of direction. Even if the composition is such that you want to position the group very close to the center of the frame, there should still be slightly more space on the side toward which the group is turned.

○ LEARNING TO IDENTIFY FORM, LINE AND DIRECTION

As you will see, designing groups depends on your sensibility of the intangible: those implied and inferred lines and shapes in a composition. Line is an artistic element used to create visual motion within the portrait. It may be implied by the arrangement of the group, or inferred, by grouping various elements within the scene.

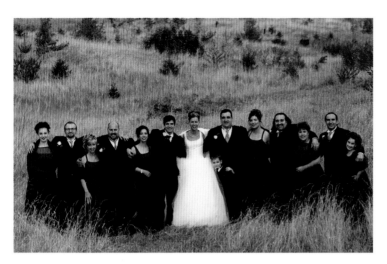

You might say this breaks the rule about groups. This group is in a straight line. None of the shoulders are turned; all face the camera. But what else is happening in this portrait? A wide sweeping S pattern follows the group from the rear of the composition, forcing your eye to follow the line and stop and examine each face in the group. Because the S curve is a recurring line, you repeat this process more than once as you look at this portrait. The spontaneity and joy in this photo match its keen design sense. Photo by Anthony Cava.

Shapes are groupings of like elements: diamond shapes, circles, pyramids, etc. These shapes are usually a collection of faces that form this type of pattern. They are used to produce pleasing shapes within the composition that guide the eye through the picture.

At first, this may be a foreign concept. But the more you learn to recognize these elements, the more they will become an integral part of your group compositions.

As in any artistic venture, the goal of the group photographer is to move the viewer's eye through the composition in an interesting way, providing the viewer with direction and movement. The opposite of this is a static image, where no motion/direction is found, and the viewer simply "recognizes" rather than enjoys all of the elements in the photo.

○ PLEASING COMPOSITIONAL FORMS

The S-shaped composition is perhaps the most pleasing of all compositions. The center of interest will fall on either a third line or a golden mean, but the remainder of the composition forms a gently sloping S shape that leads the viewer's eye to the point of main interest and through the photograph. The Z shape is a close relative to the S-shaped design.

Another pleasing form of composition is the L shape or inverted L shape, which is observed when the group's form resembles the letter L or an inverted letter L. This type of composition is ideal for reclining or seated subjects.

These compositional forms may encompass line alone or line and shape to accomplish the pattern.

○ LINE

As mentioned above, the photographer must be able to recognize real and implied lines within the photograph. A real line is one that is obvious—a horizon line, for example. An implied line is one that is not as obvious, the curve of the wrist or the bend of an arm is an implied line.

Real lines should not cut the photograph into halves. It is better to locate real lines at one-third points within the photograph.

This is important to remember about lines, real or implied: lines that meet the edge of the photograph should lead the eye into the scene and not out of it, and they should lead toward the subject. A good example of this is the country road that is widest in the foreground and narrows to a point where the subjects are walking. These lines lead the eye straight to the subjects.

Implied lines, arms and legs of the group, should not contradict the direction or emphasis of the composition, but should modify it. These lines should be gentle, not dramatic changes in direction, and again, they should lead to the main point of interest.

○ SUBJECT TONE

The eye is always drawn to the lightest part of a photograph. The rule of thumb is that light tones advance visually, dark tones retreat. It is a visual

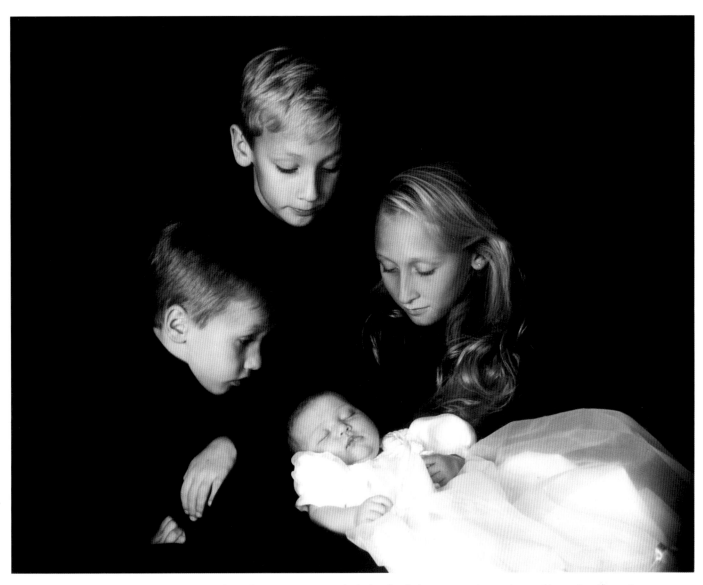

There are wonderful design elements at work in this portrait. First, the baby, the obvious center of attention, achieves visual prominence by virtue of the stark white tone of the christening dress, while all the other children are dressed in black. Secondly, the gazes of the older children, focused on the baby, are powerful implied diagonal lines leading to the baby's face. Photograph by Kimarie Richardson.

phenomenon. Therefore, elements in the picture that are lighter in tone than the subject will be distracting. Bright areas, particularly at the edges of the photograph, should be darkened either in printing, in the computer or in-camera (by masking or vignetting) so that the viewer's eye is not brought away from the subject.

There are portraits where the subject is the darkest part of the scene, such as in a high-key portrait with a white background. This is the same principle at work as above—the eye will travel to the region of greatest contrast in a field of white or on a light-colored background.

Regardless of whether the main subject is light or dark, it should dominate the rest of the photograph either by brightness or by contrast.

Whether an area is in focus or out of focus has a lot to do with the amount of visual emphasis it will receive. A light-colored background that is lighter than the group, but distinctly out of focus will not necessarily detract from the group. It may, in fact, enhance and frame the

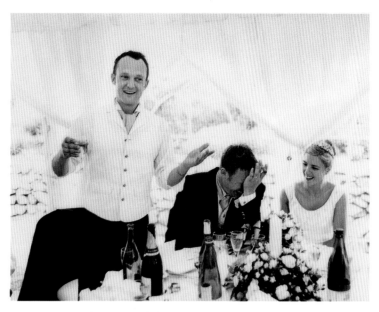

In this informal shot of the best man's toast, the photographer brightened the image to let the light tones prevail throughout. The groom, the only one dressed in solid black, thus becomes the visual center of interest. Photograph by Stephen Pugh.

group, keeping the viewer's eye centered within the group.

The same is true of foreground areas. Although it is a good idea to make them darker than your subject, sometimes you can't. If the foreground is out of focus, however, it will detract less from the group, which, hopefully, is sharp.

A technique that is becoming popular is to diffuse an area of the photograph you want to minimize or use to focus attention on your main center of interest. This is usually done in Photoshop by selecting the area and "feathering" it so that the diffusion effect diminishes the closer you get to the edge of the selection.

○ TENSION AND BALANCE

Once you begin to recognize real and implied lines and to incorporate shapes and curves into your group portraits, you need to become aware of the concepts of tension and balance. Tension is a state of imbalance in an image—a big sky and a small subject, for example, is a situation having visual tension.

Although tension does not have to be "resolved" in an image, it works together with the concept of balance so that in any given image there are elements that produce visual tension and those that produce visual balance. As you examine the photographs in this book and read the captions, you will hear these terms referred to often. Tension is often referred to as visual contrast. For example, a group of four on one side of an image and a group of two on the other side of the image produce visual tension. They contrast each other because they are different sizes and not necessarily symmetrical. But the photograph may be in a state of perfect visual balance by virtue of what falls between these two groups or for some other reason. For instance, using the same example, these two different groups could be resolved visually if the larger group is wearing dark clothes and the smaller group is wearing brighter clothes. The eye then sees the two groups as more or less equal—one group demands attention by virtue of size, the other gains attention by virtue of brightness.

These terms are subjective to a large extent, but there is no question that the eye/brain reacts favorably to both balance and visual tension and they are active ingredients in great photography.

$\mathcal{3}$

BUILDING GROUPS

There are a number of ways to look at designing groups. The first is a technical aspect. Design your group so that those posed in the back are as close as possible to those in the front. This ensures that your plane of focus will cover the front row as well as the back row. It is a good habit to get into if you want your groups to be sharply focused.

. . . sometimes the design itself can be what's important.

The second consideration in designing groups is aesthetic. You are building a design when creating a group portrait. Norman Phillips likens group design to a florist arranging flowers. He says, "Sometimes we might want a tight bouquet of faces. Other times we might want to arrange our subjects so that the group looks interesting apart from the dynamics of the people in the group." In other words, sometimes the design itself can be what's important.

A third consideration is proximity. How close do you want each member of the group to be? Phillips relates proximity to warmth and distance to elegance. If you open the group up you have a lot more freedom to introduce flowing lines and shapes within the composition of the group. A tightly arranged group where members are touching implies warmth and closeness.

○ POSING HIERARCHY

Is it more important to pose by age, importance or by size? This is a question of considerable debate among group portrait photographers. Some advise photographers to concentrate on organizing the groups and subgroups into logical units. The reasoning is that these subgroups (such as the oldest son, his wife and two kids), want to be photographed separately at the same session, thus doubling sales. Also, the family is more cohesively arranged if organized by age (grandparents in the middle, with their children adjacent and the grandchildren and their families in the outer realms of the group). One can arrange subjects by size within the subgroups for the most pleasing composition.

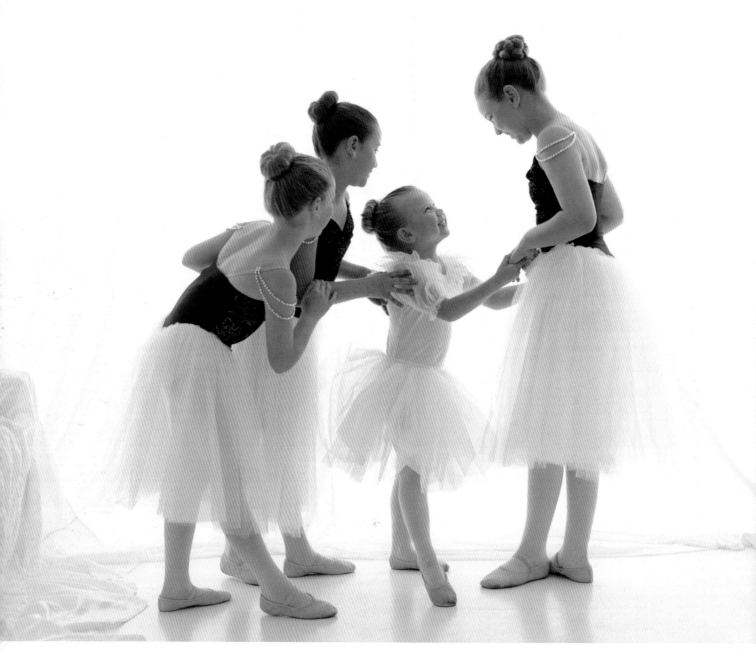

How close you want each subject to one another is a function of how you design the group. Separating your subjects so that you can create a pleasant array of lines and shapes leads to an elegant image such as this one. Here, the tiny ballerina is the focus of the portrait and the others form an implied and very graceful circle around her. Notice too how the draped background supports the design of this image. Photograph by Norman Phillips.

Sometimes, as Norman Phillips likes to say, you might design the photo to attain a "tight bouquet of faces," as was done here. These beautiful faces needed to be seen close up. Dressing them in black and only allowing one hand to show in the pose focuses all of the viewer's attention on the faces. Although their eye and head height is identical, not something that you generally want to do, it is effective in conveying their closeness. Photograph by Norman Phillips.

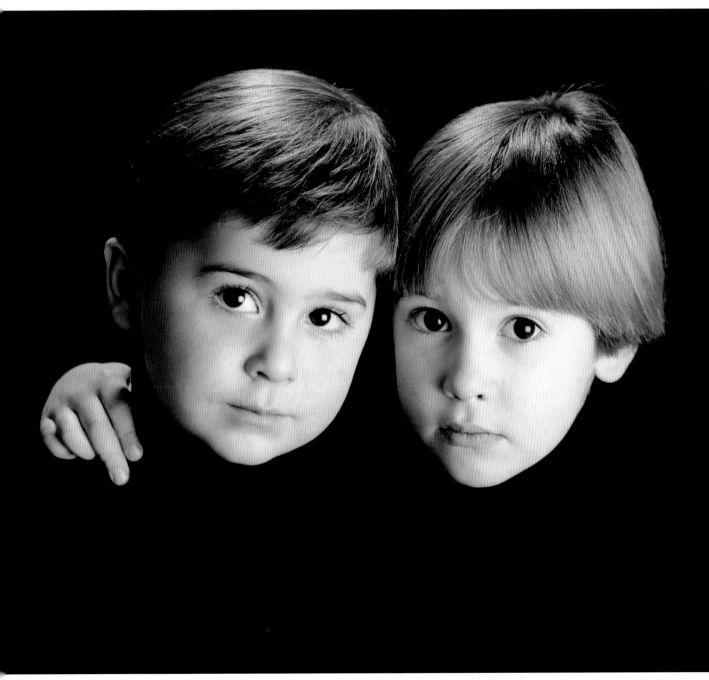

Many photographers feel that posing by size and shape creates by far the most interesting and attractively posed group. This is certainly true for weddings, where groups, formal or informal, can be arranged in any number of ways as long as the bride and groom are center-most. This method also affords the photographer the most flexibility to hide and flatter individual members of the group.

Some photographers pose their groups from the center out. In the case of a family group, the grandparents or parents would be right in the middle. Other photographers prefer to pose their groups by defining the perimeters of the group (i.e., the frame edges, left and right), and then filling in the center with interesting groupings.

○ POSING DIALOGUE

It is always better to *show* than it is to *tell* your subjects how you want them to pose. Always act out how you want the person to pose. It's much easier than describing what you want and it takes less time. Once they're in the pose you want, wait for the special moment when they forget all about having their pictures taken. Then it's show time.

As mentioned above, always be positive and always be in charge. Once you lose control of a large group it's difficult or impossible to regain.

Talk to your subjects and tell them how good they look and that you can feel their special emotion (whatever dialogue seems appropriate). Let them know that you appreciate them as unique individuals, and so on. If closeness is what you are after, talk them into it. It sounds hokey, but if it does nothing more than relax your subjects, you have done a good thing.

○ PERIMETER CHECK

Once your group is composed and especially when working with larger groups, do your once-around-the-frame analysis, making sure poses, lighting and expressions are good and that nothing needs

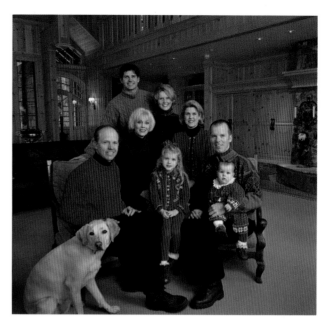

Sometimes you will want to pose a family using established hierarchies, in this case by family group. The parents are center-most. Their kids plus spouses are arranged behind the parents, but the two families are separate. Husbands and wives are posed together. Notice how the photographer captured the room light and the beautiful wood interior of the home. By using a wide-angle lens and positioning the group far from the background, the photographer made the people dominant in the scene. Photograph by Robert Love.

adjusting. You should not only check each person in the group in the viewfinder, but once that's done, check the negative space around each person. Scan the perimeter of each person, checking for obvious flaws and refinements you could quickly make. Now is the time to analyze your image, not after you've made four or five frames. Learn to check the viewfinder quickly. Two quick scans are all it takes.

○ COORDINATING APPAREL

Sometimes the group composition will be dictated by what the people are wearing.

It sounds so easy. The outdoors is yours for making a family group portrait. Just go outside to the backyard, to the beach, to a park or by a lake; have everyone dress casually, and take the picture. For the most part, that is all you're going to get, a picture.

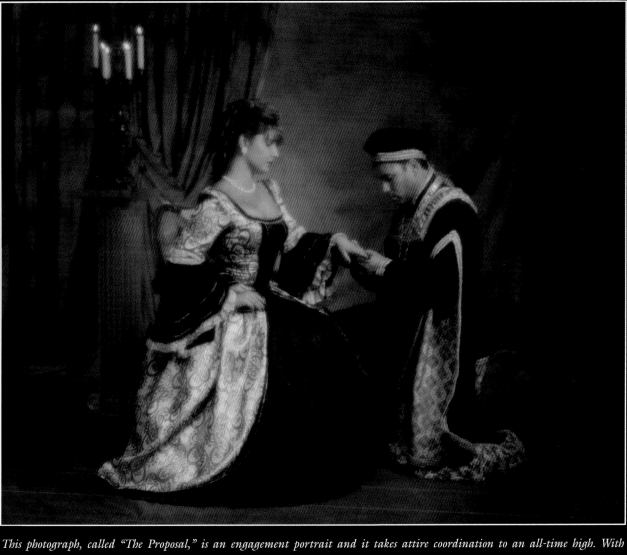

This photograph, called "The Proposal," is an engagement portrait and it takes attire coordination to an all-time high. With costuming, lighting and propping all consistent, the photographer used a series of amber and red gels to make the image look like it was lit by candlelight. The profile posing is elegant and effective. Note how space is visible on either side of the seated woman to slim her waist. Note also that both bodies are at 45-degree angles to one another to best support the profile poses. Photograph by Robert Lino.

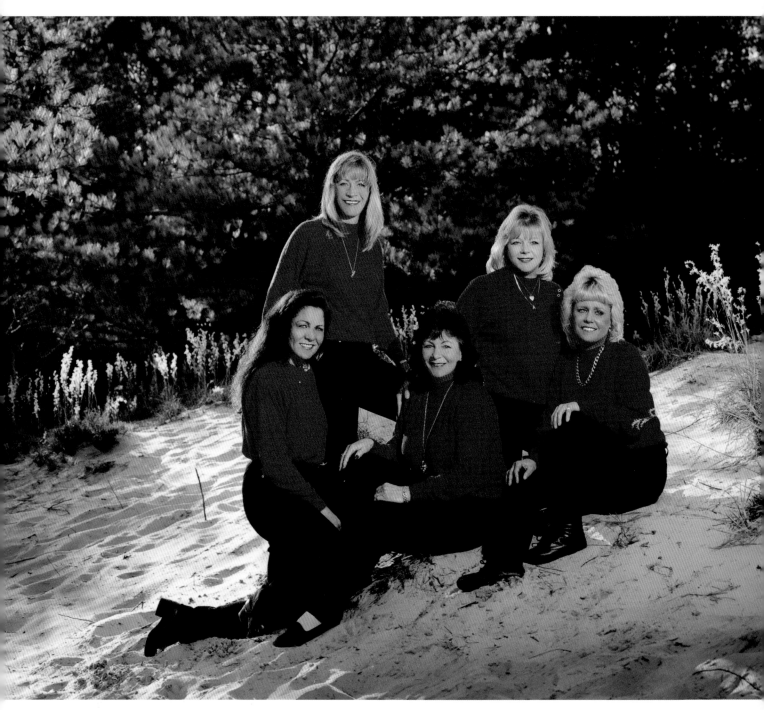

The oldest daughter consulted with photographer Bill McIntosh on a portrait for her mother's birthday. She wanted her three sisters and herself with her mother in the portrait in an outdoor setting. They discussed the clothing and location. She bought red sweaters for mom and a sister that did not have one and Bill recommended a location on the side of a sand dune in the afternoon, when the sun was behind the dunes. Bill used a Lumedyne strobe at the same exposure as the daylight to light the group. McIntosh used a Mamiya RZ 67 with 110mm lens and Fujifilm NPH 400. The exposure was ½₅ at f/11. McIntosh likes to use the sun as a backlight— it makes the subjects stand out and adds saturation to the portrait. Note that this group is a somewhat standard grouping—three in the front, two in the back. Photograph by Bill McIntosh.

One noted photographer, who shall remain nameless, says "They never listen to me no matter how adamant I am about coordinating the clothes. I am constantly amazed at what they show up in."

Others, like Bill McIntosh, are masters of the coordinated environment. Here's what he has to say about planning. "No matter how good your artistic and photographic skills are, there is one more element required to make a great portrait—color harmony. In McIntosh's photographs the style and color of the clothing all coordinate. He says, "I have ensured these suit both the subjects and the environment chosen." Bill makes sure everything matches. "Time is well spent before the sitting discussing the style of clothing—formal or casual—and then advising clients of particular colors which they feel happy with and which would also create a harmonious portrait."

Some photographers view clothes and their harmony as the primary element in the fine group portrait. Clothes should be coordinated for color, tone and style. Take, for example, an uncoordinated group where some are wearing short sleeves, some long; some are wearing light-colored pants and skirts, others dark; some have brown shoes, others white; and each person is wearing a different color and pattern. The result will be a cacophony of styles and you are going to capture an unattractive portrait, regardless of how good the lighting and composition are.

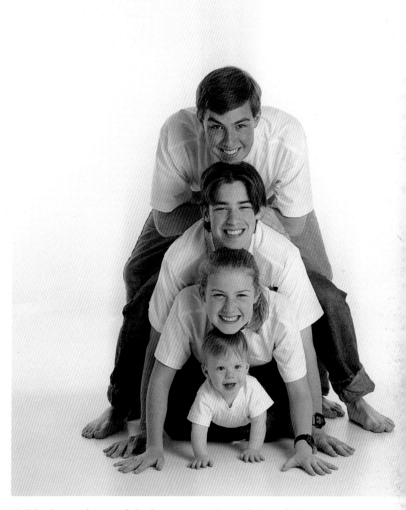

Solid colors and neutral shades are part of a good formula for success. The attire was kept simple and the pose, even simpler. It is usually not advisable to have heads atop other heads. However, here, the photographer breaks that rule with authority, opting for a close and fun family pose. Photograph by Norman Phillips.

○ Photographers' Favorites

White is a photographer's favorite, provided the subjects are of average weight or slender. If your group is on the large side, all that white will make necks and torsos look much larger than they really are. The general rule of thumb is wear white or pastel, you gain ten pounds; wear dark or medium shades, you lose ten pounds.

Solid-colored clothes, in cool or neutral shades, with long sleeves, always look good. Cool colors, such as blue and green, recede, while warm colors,

such as red, orange and yellow, advance. Cool colors or neutral colors (such as black, white and gray) will emphasize the faces and make them appear warmer and more pleasing in the photographs.

Your group's garments should blend. For example, all of the family-group members should wear informal or formal outfits. It's easy when photographing the wedding party when all are dressed identically and formally. Half your battle is

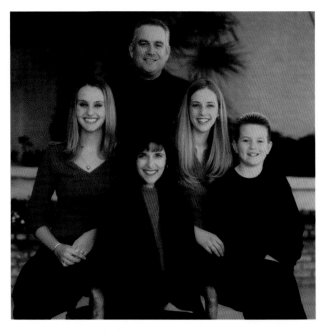

Right: The armchair, barely visible, is the basis for this attractive pyramid-shaped portrait. Mom, seated, is moved far forward on the chair for the best posture. The daughters—one on each arm—are positioned behind mom, helping to form the base of the pyramid. The young son is leaning in—not seated or standing—but the overall pose is effective. Notice the diamond-shape to the four central figures, with the fifth member elongating one edge of the pyramid shape. Photograph by Kenneth Sklute. Bottom: Here is an extended use of the armchair—two armchairs, with both arms being used to create new levels for the group. Notice how bodies overlap to help slim and shape the women in the group. Notice too how hands are either hidden or posed—a good lesson for groups of any size. The bride stands out beautifully because everything about the pose is used to modify her position in the picture. Photograph by Kenneth Sklute.

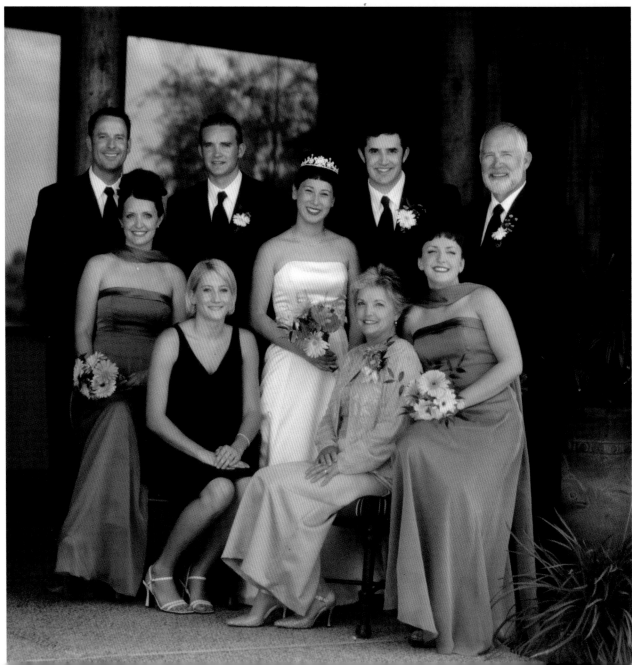

won. It is difficult to pose a group when some people are wearing suits and ties and others are wearing jeans and polo shirts. Shoe styles and colors should blend with the rest of a person's attire: dark outfits call for dark shoes and socks.

Robert Love boils it down to this: "Color coordination is the main reason that people do not like their previous family portraits." In his pre-session consultation, he talks about color coordination and recommends solid colors, long sleeves and V-necks for the most flattering portraits.

○ THE ARMCHAIR

Once you begin adding people to a group, one of your preeminent props will be the stuffed armchair, small sofa or love seat. Its wide arms and often attractively upholstered surface is ideal for supporting additional group members.

An armchair is usually positioned at about 30 to 45 degrees to the camera. Regardless of who will occupy the seat, he and/or she should be seated at an angle to the camera. They should be seated on the edge of the chair, so that all of their weight does not rest on the chair back. This promotes good sitting posture and slims the lines of the waist and hips, for both men and women.

You will more than likely have to straighten out seated men's jackets and ask the women to straighten the line of their dresses, as sitting normally causes dresses and coats to ride up and bunch.

Here's how Monte Zucker uses an armchair to build a group of almost any size. A woman sits with the upper part of her legs following in the direction that her body is facing. Her legs are then bent back and her ankles crossed. A man sits similarly, except that his feet aren't crossed. The foot closest to the camera is pointed toward the lens, while the other foot is positioned at almost a right angle to the front foot.

For a group of two, you can seat one person and either stand the second person facing the chair (for a full-length picture), or seat the second person on the arm of the chair, facing inward toward the person seated in the chair. The body of the person seated in the chair should be in front of the person seated on the arm.

When adding a third person to the group, you can either seat the person on the arm or stand the person. That person should have his/her weight on the back foot, lowering the back shoulder. All three heads should be equidistant.

A group of four has two people seated in chairs, one person seated on the arm, facing inward toward the center of the group. The fourth person is standing, facing toward the center of the group. The person seated on the arm of the chair has his arm coming straight down behind the person seated slightly in front of him. In all groups there should be equal distance between each of the heads. Do not have two heads close together, while the others are spaced farther apart. It destroys the rhythm of the group.

If there is a heavy person, put that person behind someone, so that you are covering some of his or her body. Make certain that all the people seated on the arms are behind the people seated in the chairs.

From here on, it's just a question of adding faces where they need to be to continue the flow of the composition. You can fit someone squatted down in the middle of the group, covering a lot of legs. You can have people kneel down on either side of the group as well as seated on the ground, completing the pyramid composition. This little group can easily become a group of fourteen. Just follow the rhythm throughout the group. Look for the triangles between heads, diagonal lines and equal spacing between all of the people.

○ START WITH TWO

The simplest of groups is two people. Whether the group is a bride and groom, brothers and sisters or grandma and grandpa, the basic building blocks call for one person slightly higher than the other. Generally speaking, the mouth height of the higher subject should be at the forehead height of the lower subject. Many photogra-

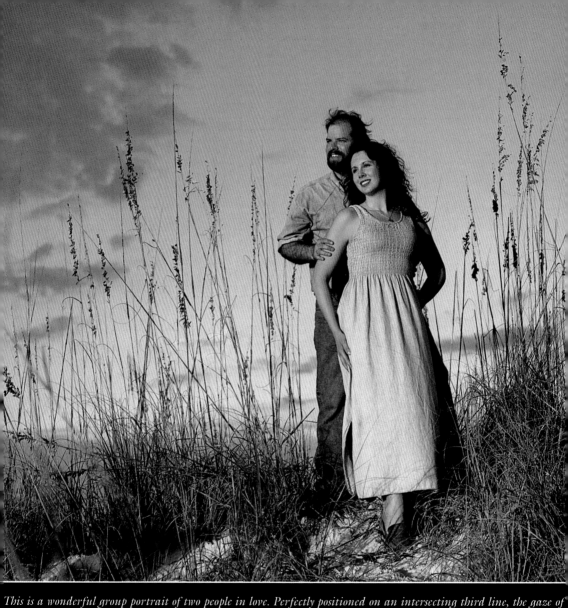

This is a wonderful group portrait of two people in love. Perfectly positioned on an intersecting third line, the gaze of the couple forces the direction of the portrait camera left. In order to give the couple a base, the photographer had the man spread his feet outside the form of the woman. Notice the cloud in the upper left that perfectly balances the form of the couple. And notice too the space at the woman's waist created by the posing of her hands—a slimming, form-flattering pose. Photographed by direct sunlight, late in the day with no fill. Photograph by Monte Zucker.

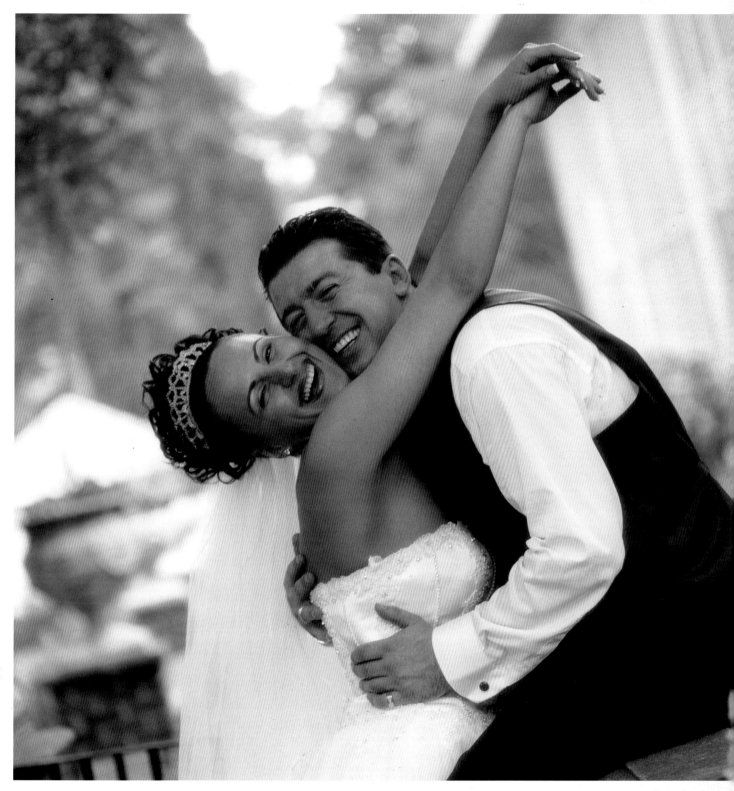

This is an intimate, joyous portrait made on the day of the wedding. The photographer, to kick-start the dynamics of the image, tilted the camera to produce a diagonal image, which immediately focuses attention on the slanted faces. This effect would not have been possible without very shallow depth of field, which completely softens the background. One fine point to notice is the delicate line and pose of the woman's hands. It is a dynamic line that demands your visual attention. Photograph by Vladimir Bekker.

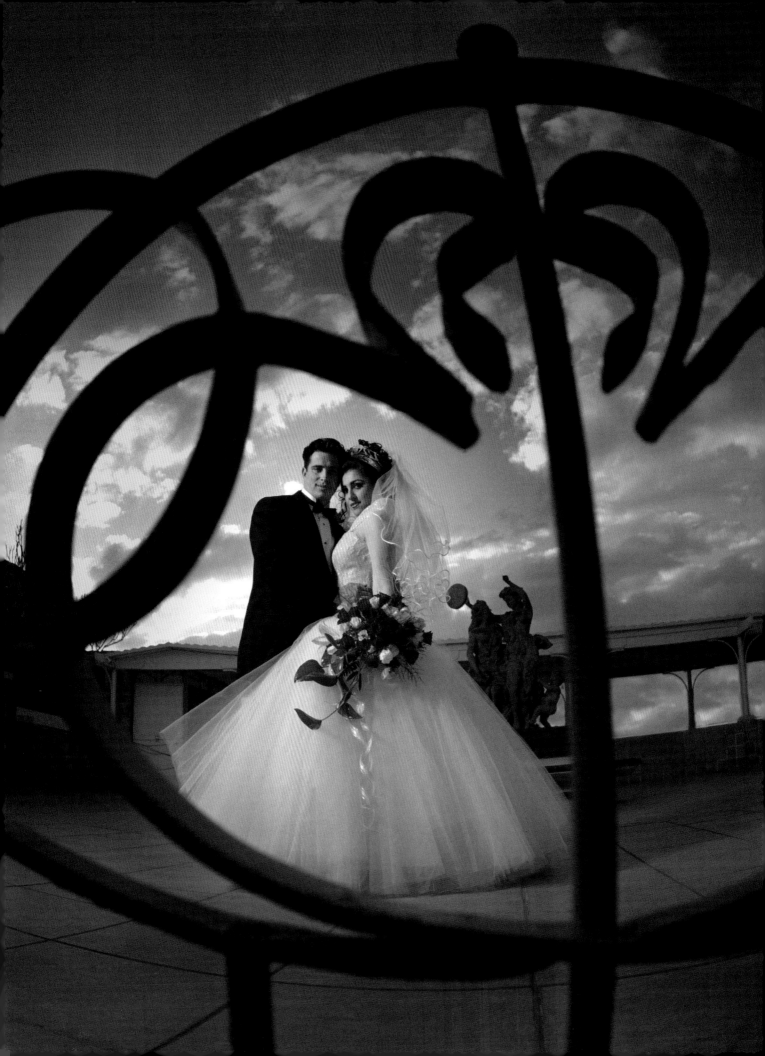

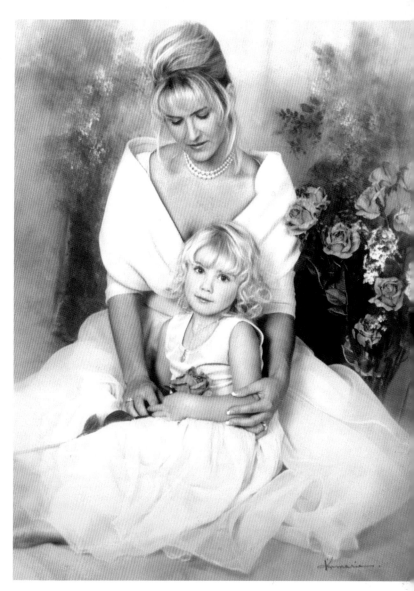

phers recommend mouth to eyes as the ideal starting point.

Although they can be posed in a parallel position, each with their shoulders and heads turned the same direction, as one might do with twins, for example—a more interesting dynamic can be achieved by having them pose at 45-degree angles to each other so their shoulders face in toward one another. With this pose you can create a number of variations by moving them closer or farther apart.

Another intimate pose for two is to have two profiles facing each other. One should still be higher than the other, to allow you to create an implied diagonal line between their eyes, which also gives the portrait direction.

Since this type of image will be fairly close up, you will want to make sure that the frontal planes of their faces are roughly parallel so that you can hold the focus in both faces.

Using an armchair allows you to seat one person, usually the woman, and position the other person close and on the arm of the chair, leaning on the far armrest. This puts their faces in close proximity but at different heights.

A variation of this is to have the woman seated and the man standing. However, when their heads are so far apart, you should pull back and make the portrait full-length.

When you seat the woman in an armchair, her hands should be in her lap and used to slim the body—waist, thighs and hips. She should be seated at an angle and the leg farthest from the camera should have that foot "hooked" behind the front leg—a pose that women seem to fall into naturally.

For as many examples as are given here, there are ten times as many variations. Study groups of two as there are some very dynamic ways to pose two people, only a handful of which are covered here.

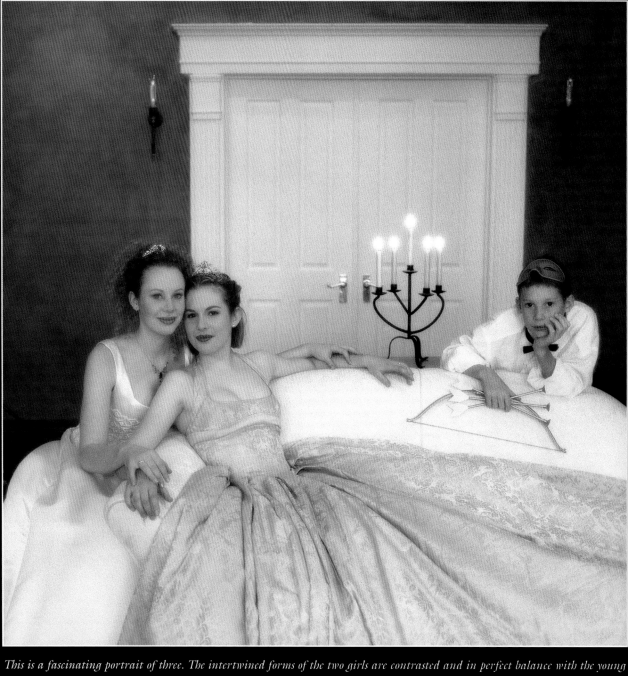

This is a fascinating portrait of three. The intertwined forms of the two girls are contrasted and in perfect balance with the young boy with the bow and arrow. The candelabra provides a stopping point for the eye—you cannot go back and forth between the subjects without seeing it. The stately elegance and starkness of the room only underscores the sense of mystery in this portrait. Photograph by David Anthony Williams.

○ ADD A THIRD

A group portrait of three is still small and intimate. It lends itself to a pyramid or diamond-shaped composition, or an inverted triangle, all of which are pleasing to the eye.

Don't simply adjust the height of the faces so that each is at a different level. Use the turn of the shoulders of those at either end of the group as a means of looping the group together.

Once you add a third person, you will begin to notice the interplay of lines and shapes inherent in good group design. As an exercise, plot the implied line that goes through the shoulders or faces of the three people in the group. If the line is sharp or jagged, try adjusting the composition so that the line is more flowing, with gentler angles. Try a simple maneuver like turning the last or lowest person in the group inward toward the group and see what effect it has.

Still as part of the exercise, try a different configuration. For example, create a single diagonal line with the faces at different heights and all people in the group touching. It's a simple yet very pleasing design. The power and serenity of a well-defined diagonal line in a composition can compel the viewer to keep looking at the portrait. Adjust the group again by having those at the ends of the diagonal tilt their heads slightly in toward the center person. It's a slight adjustment that can make all the difference.

How about trying the bird's-eye view? Cluster the group of three together, grab a stepladder or other high vantage point and you've got a lovely variation on the three-person group.

One of Monte Zucker's favorites for doing quick three-person groups at wedding receptions is to have one person seated with two people standing behind, leaning down so that their heads are in close proximity to the seated person's head. It's a shot he can make quickly and all the faces are in the same plane, so sharp focus is easily attained.

When you add a third person to the group, hands and legs start to become a problem. One solution is to show only one arm and leg per person. This is sage advice, especially when the group is similarly dressed. One is not always sure whose hand belongs to whom. Generally, the outer hand should be visible, the inner hand, compositionally, can be easily hidden.

Groups of three and more allow the photographer to draw on more of the available elements of design, in addition to the design elements of the group itself. The accomplished group photographer will incorporate architectural compo-

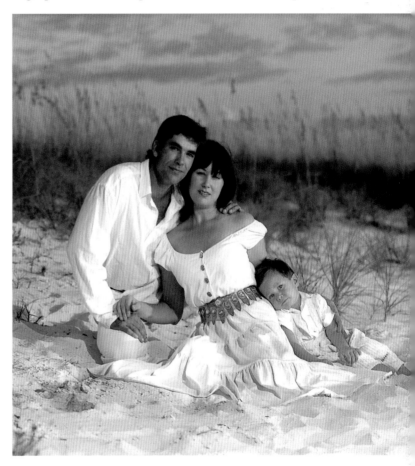

A perfect white pyramid is formed with this elegant grouping of three. The pose is formal and yet there is great intimacy and warmth here. Notice how the line of the boy was used to lengthen the shape of the pyramid, and all three faces are in line but at slightly different angles. Note too how the woman has rolled her weight onto the side of her right leg, partially to extend the pose, partially to create a more flattering, slimming look. Photograph by Monte Zucker.

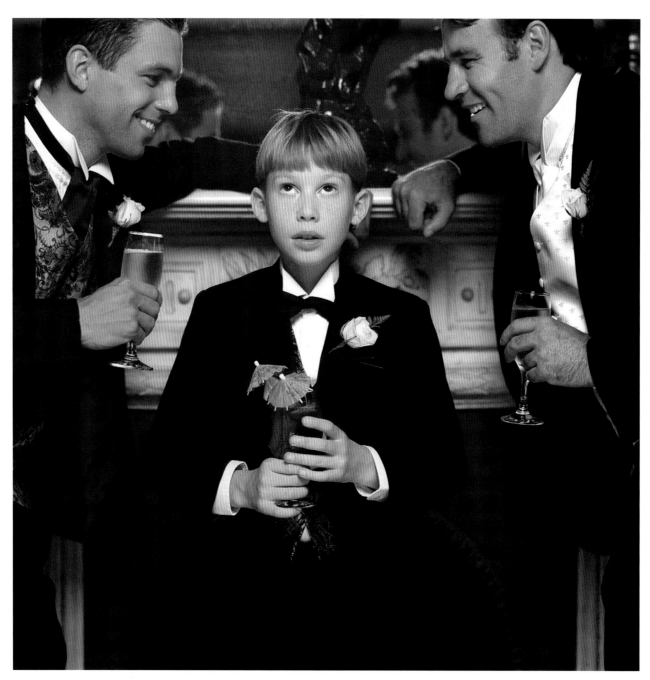

Above: This storytelling portrait depends on close cropping and expressions to communicate its message. This image was part of a series done for Kodak Professional Australia. The young boy is "caught in the act" by the understanding stare-down of the men who bracket him. The cropping of the tops of heads would not ordinarily be done in group portraiture, but here it is an effective means of focusing attention on the boy. The composition is an inverted pyramid shape. Photograph by David Williams. **Opposite:** "Valley Girls" was a shot that was literally thrown together on two days' notice for the Los Angeles Times. Rather than stick with a "safe" shoot with just one model, the photographer chose to work with four! The shot began by coordinating the outfits. The ladies agreed on black for a tight look that would pull them together as a group. The posing was partially dictated by the lighting and f-stop (f/11) chosen. The camera would need to be fairly close to the subjects to frame the tight portrait. The faces had to be close to the same plane to ensure that each girl's eyes were sharp. The dark backdrop was lit with a red gel to play off the black wardrobe and add some zest to the shot. The main light was a 30x40-inch Photoflex softbox. Various fill, hair and background lights were also used. Photograph by Stephen Dantzig.

nents, or natural elements, such as hills, trees, shrubs, flowers, gates, archways, furniture, etc.

As you add more people to a group, remember to do everything you can to keep the film plane parallel to the plane of the group to ensure everyone in the photograph is sharply focused.

○ ADDING A FOURTH

Now is when things get interesting. You will find that as you photograph more group portraits even numbers of people are harder to pose than odd. Three, five, seven or nine people are much easier to photograph than the even-numbered group of

subjects. The reason is that the eye and brain tend to accept the disorder of odd-numbered objects more readily than even-numbered objects. As you will see, the fourth member of a group can become an "extra wheel" if not handled properly. According to Norman Phillips, even numbers don't work as well because they make diagonals too long and they leave an extra person to find space for in traditional triangular compositions.

With four people, you can simply add a person to the existing poses of three described above, with the following caveat. Be sure to keep the eye height of the fourth person different from any of

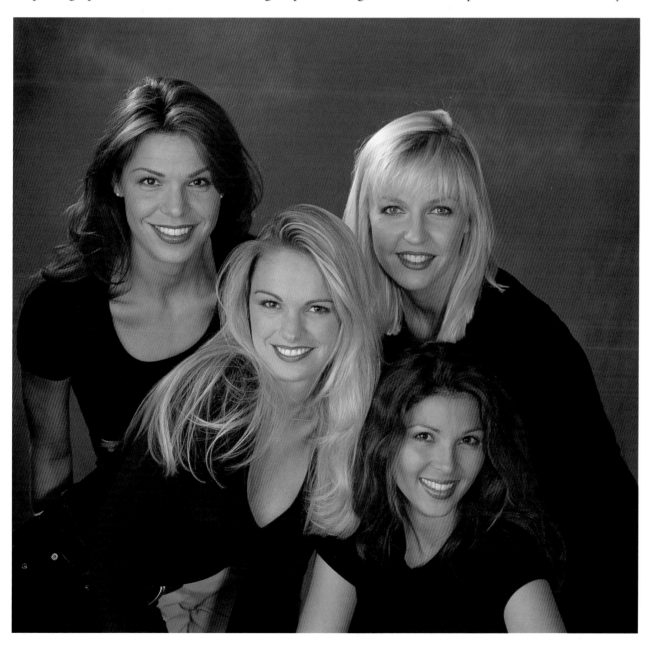

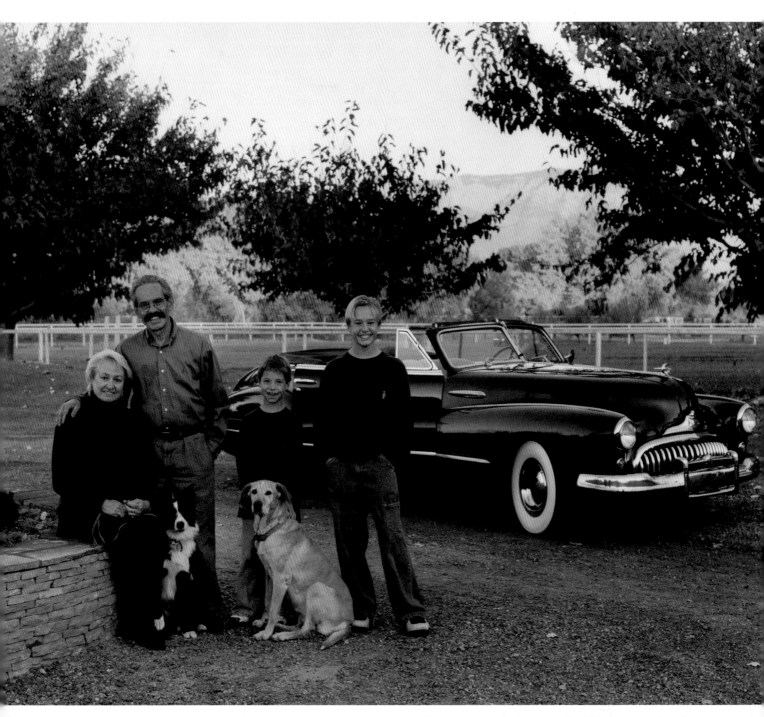

When a family is photographed with a prized possession, in this case, the antique Buick, the posing should loosen up so that the group relates visually to the item of value. Here, there is plenty of space between the boys so the car is visible between them. The photographer chose to hide as many hands as possible and position the family in the lower third of the image, allowing the Buick to achieve some visual prominence. Even with the beautiful open highlights (by the way, this is done just the way they do it in Detroit) on the car and the golden leaves in the background, the group is still the visual center of interest in this carefully crafted portrait. The reason for the group's visual prominence in this photo is the use of a slight wide-angle lens and the extended distance between the subjects and the car. The closer the camera and lens are to the group, the more the people will be the predominant subject. Photograph by Frank Frost.

This family is in deep shade with some sun coming through the trees behind them. The meter reading was ¹⁄₆₀ at f/8. The photographer slowed down the shutter speed to ¹⁄₃₀ to get a good exposure for the background. It requires one stop more exposure in shade, to compensate for the loss of red light when making portraits in the shade. A Lumedyne barebulb strobe exposure was set for f/8. Camera: Mamiya RZ 67 with 110mm lens. Film: Fuji NHG II 800 film. The fourth member of the group, the one outside the basic triangle shape, is a large enough figure to balance the other three visually, for a well-balanced group portrait. The use of white clothing for all group members is the photographer's favorite. Notice the similarity between this pose and the one on page 63. Photograph by Bill McIntosh.

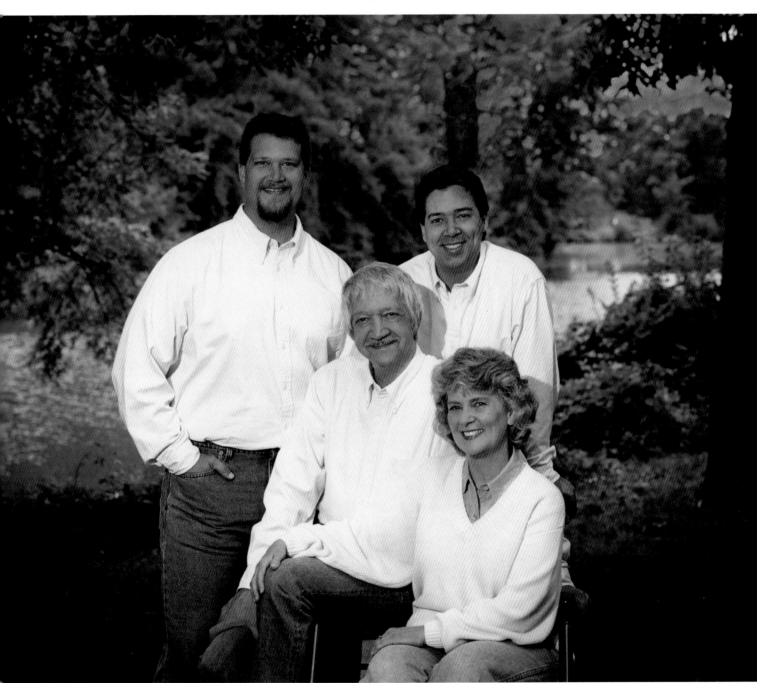

the others in the group. Also, be aware that you are now forming shapes within your composition. Try to think in terms of pyramids, inverted triangles, diamonds and curved lines.

The various body parts—for instance the line up one arm, through the shoulders of several people and down the arm of the person on the far side of the group—form an implied line that is just as important as the shapes you define with faces. Be aware of both line and shape—and direction—as you build your groups.

An excellent pose for four people is the sweeping curve of three people with the fourth person added below and between the first and second person in the group.

If you find that one of your subjects in your group is not dressed the same as the others (this happens more than you would imagine), he or she can be positioned slightly outside the group for accent, without necessarily disrupting the color harmony of the rest of the group (see page 68).

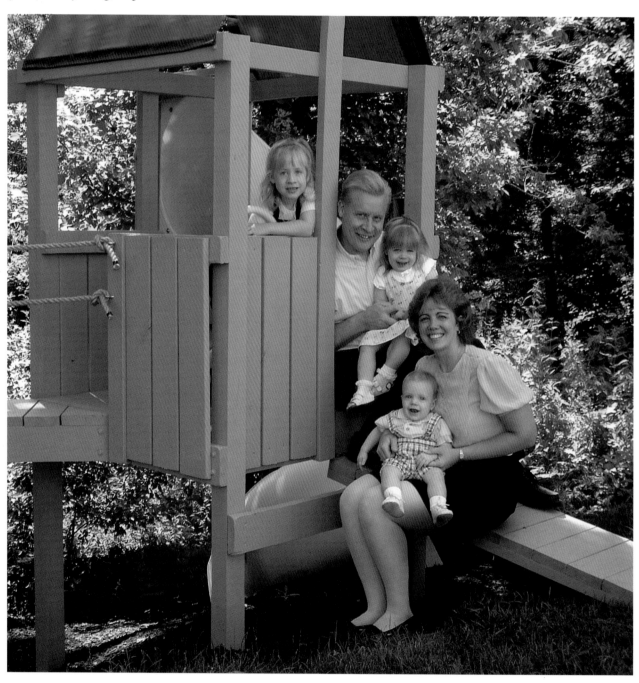

This is a lovely self-portrait of the Michael Ayers family done on some backyard play equipment, which provided a lovely C-curve composition. The gently sloping curve of the composition takes you from person to person up and down the group. It is a very effective means of designing medium-sized groups. Photograph by Michael Ayers.

When Monte has to pose four people, he sometimes prefers to play off of the symmetry of the even number of people. He'll break the rules and he'll seat two and stand two and, with heads close together, make the line of the eyes of the two people parallel with the eyes of the bottom two.

When two of the four are little people, they can be "draped" to either side of the adults to form one of the pleasing traditional shapes.

○ FIVE ON UP

Remember that the composition will always look better if the base is wider than the top, so the final person should elongate the bottom of the group.

Remember too that each implied line and shape in the photograph should be designed by you and should be intentional. If it isn't logical—i.e., the line or shape doesn't make sense visually—then move people around and start again. The viewer's eye should not just be meandering through the image, but guided by the lines and shapes you create within the composition.

Try to coax S shapes and Z shapes out of your compositions. They form the most pleasing shapes to the eye and will hold a viewer's eye within the borders of the print.

Remember that the diagonal line has a great deal of visual power in an image and is one of the most potent design tools at your disposal.

Always remember that the use of different levels creates a sense of visual interest and lets the viewer's eye bounce from one face to another (as long as there is a logical and pleasing flow to the arrangement). The placement of faces, not bodies, dictates how pleasing and effective a composition will be.

When adding a sixth or an eighth person to the group, the group still must look asymmetrical for best effect. This is best accomplished by elongating sweeping lines and using the increased space to slot extra people. Keep in mind that while a triangle shape normally calls for three people,

you can add a fourth subject and keep the shape intact.

As your groups get bigger, keep your depth of field under control. Use the tricks described earlier (like raising the camera to keep it parallel to the group or leaning the last row in and the front row back slightly to create a shallower subject plane).

As you add people to the group beyond six, you should start to base the shapes within the composition on linked shapes, like linked circles or

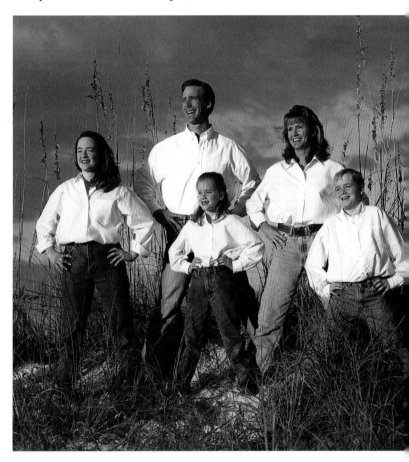

A fun pose, along with great outfit coordination and great expressions make this a terrific family portrait. Notice how all faces are at different levels and the pose has a strong horizontal base, created by moving the children to the front. This pose is made more effective by loosening it up and creating some space between family members. Again, this is a basic pose—three in front and two in back. Photograph by Monte Zucker.

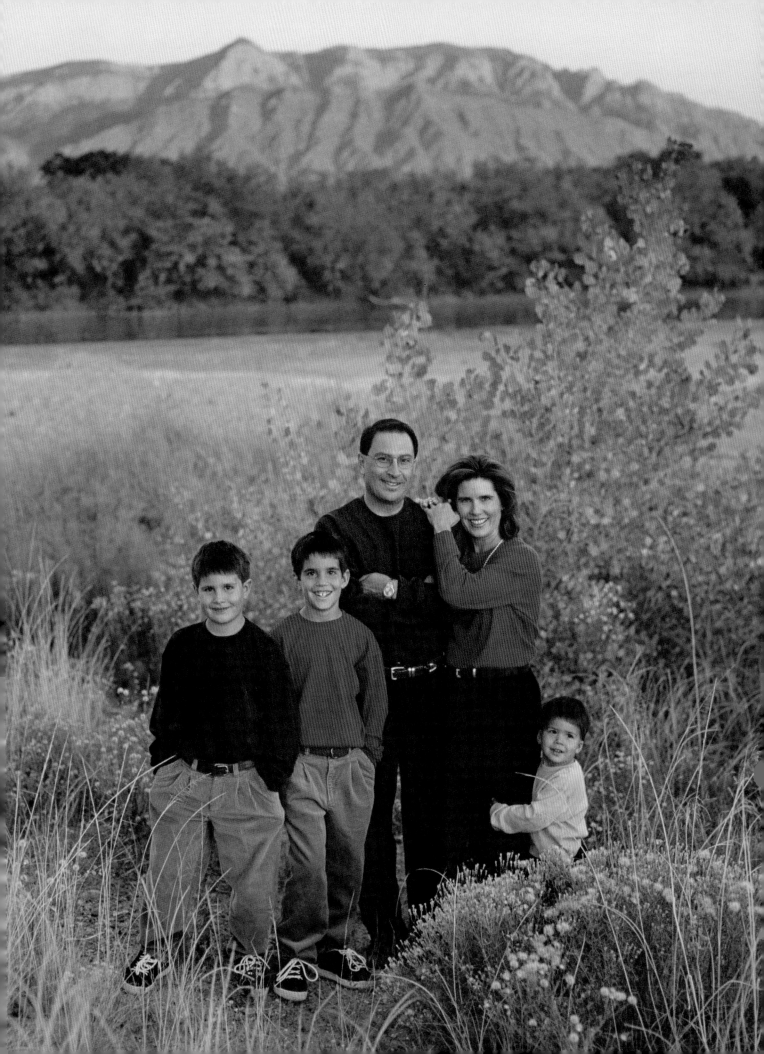

Opposite: This is a beautiful environmental portrait. The use of red and black alternating shirts produces a bold ricochet effect, and the touch of yellow on the little guy on the right makes him a "sparkling jewel" in the lower portion of the composition. The little guy on the right, because he is dressed in gold, which is much brighter than either red or black, balances the two much larger vertical shapes—the two brothers, the mom and the dad. Photograph by Frank Frost.

triangles. What makes the combined shapes work is to turn them toward the center—the diamond shape of four on the left can be turned 20 degrees or less toward center, the diamond shape of four on the right (which may encompass the middle-most person from the other group) can also be turned toward the center.

○ OBVIOUS THINGS TO AVOID

One of the biggest flaws a photographer can make in an image is a background element that seemingly "sprouts" from one of the subjects. The classic telephone pole comes to mind. While this is an amateur mistake for the most part, the truth is that I see an amazing number of prints from proven and sometimes award-winning pros that make this same mistake. The problem is that the photographer fails to do a final perimeter check. Again, that's where you scan the subject's silhouette, making sure there's nothing in the background that you missed. Pay particular attention to strong verticals, like light-colored posts or columns, and also diagonals. Even though these elements may be out of focus, if they are tonally dominant they will disrupt and often ruin an otherwise beautiful composition.

One way to control your background more effectively is to scout the locations you want to use before you show up to make the portrait. Check the light at the right time of day and be prepared for what the changing light might do to your background an hour or two later.

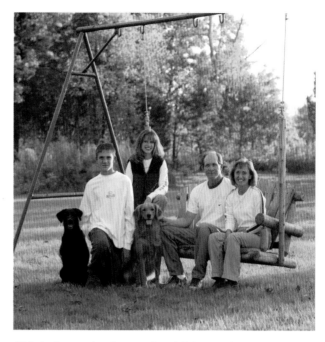

This is the one the photographer didn't see. The "noose" behind the head of the second subject is probably not what this family had in mind when they hired the photographer for a group portrait. A perimeter check in the viewfinder around each person in your image will prevent this kind of problem. Photograph by Michael Ayers.

BUILDING BIG GROUPS

Once a group exceeds nine people, it is no longer a small group. The complexities of posing and lighting expand and, if you're not careful to stay in charge, chaos will reign. It is always best to have a game plan in mind with big groups.

It is always best to have a game plan in mind with big groups.

Posing bigger groups requires you to use standing poses, often combined with sitting and kneeling poses. Those standing should be turned at least 20 degrees off center so that their shoulders are not parallel to the film plane. The exception is with small children who gain visual prominence when they are square to the camera.

With standing poses, care must be taken to disguise wide hips and torsos, which can sometimes be accomplished simply by using other people in the group. Always create space between the arms and torso simply by placing a hand on a hip or, in the case of men, placing a hand in a pocket (thumb out).

In really large groups, clothing coordination can be a nightmare. It is often best to divide the group into subgroups—family units, for instance—and have them coordinate with each other. For example, a family in khaki pants and yellow sweaters could be positioned next to a family in blue jeans and red sweaters.

○ NATURALNESS COUNTS

It is important with medium to large-size groups that the poses you put your subjects in appear to be natural and comfortable. Even experienced group photographers working with assistants will take ten minutes or so to set up a group of twenty or more. Therefore, it is imperative that your subjects be posed comfortably. Natural poses, ones that your subjects might fall into without prompting, are best and can be held indefinitely.

It is important that the group remains alert and in tune with what you are doing. Here is where it is important to stay in charge of the posing. The loudest voice—the one that people are listening to—should be yours, although by no means should you be yelling at your group. Instead, be assertive and positive and act in control.

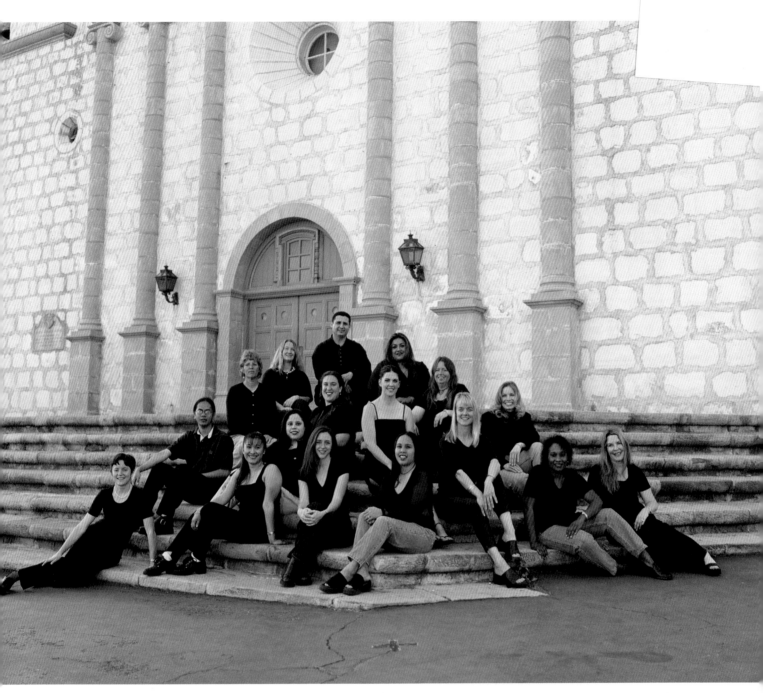

Big groups mean big problems, not the least of which is uniformity. In this group portrait of nurses made at the Santa Barbara Mission, the dress code was black and, naturally, five showed up in jeans. The photographer did what any portrait artist would do—hide two and form a triangle within the composition with the other three. In order to "spread" the pyramid, the photographer created longer, more sweeping poses to elongate the base of the pyramid shape. The expressions are flawless, as is the lighting. A broad, flawless light source (the southern sky) illuminated each person in the group without the need for a supplemental fill-in light source. Photograph by Heidi Mauracher.

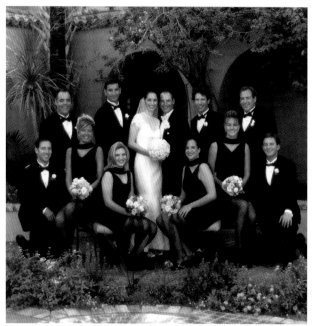

Left: *This elegant bridal group uses three levels: two levels of seated figures, one level of standing-kneel figures, and a level of standing figures. Try to find the shapes and lines at work here. X-shaped patterns of overlapping diagonal lines crisscross the bridal party on both sides of the bride and groom. Both groups are angled in to draw your eye to the couple. The background and foreground are elegant and subdued. Photograph by Kenneth Sklute.* **Below:** *Multiple levels and overlapping shapes define this fine family portrait. The group to the left seems disconnected from the seated group to the right until you realize there is a subtle diagonal connecting the two groups. Also, you can follow the line of black sweaters from left to right. Note the creative use of levels in the group on the right and the all-standing pose on the left—contrast and balance. Photograph by Norman Phillips.*

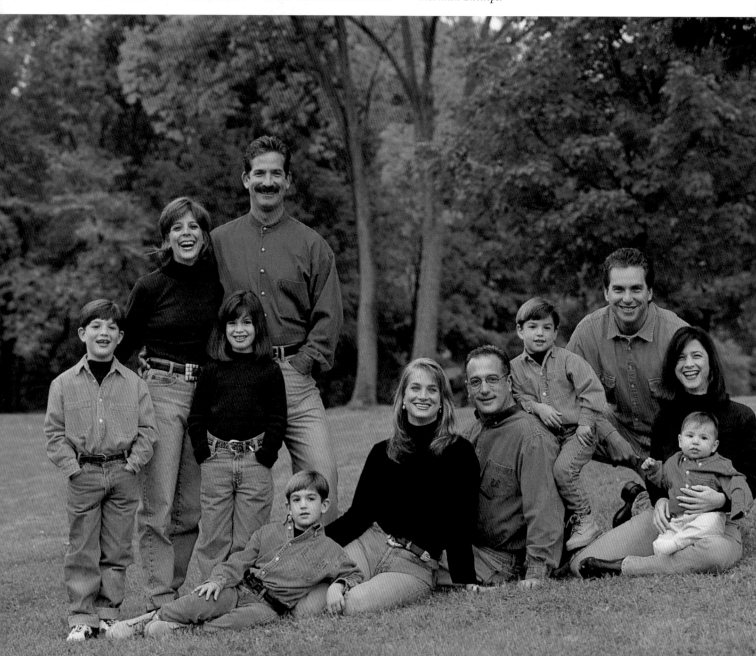

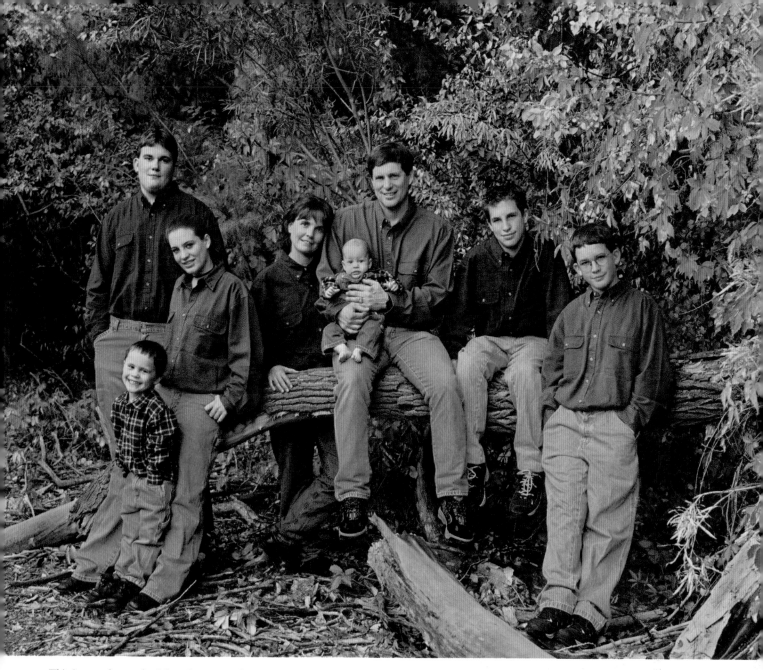

This is a truly wonderful environmental group portrait. First note the lead-in line of the foreground log that draws your eye to the group. There is a subgroup of three figures on the left that form a gentle "C" shape, and a subgroup on the right, which forms a pleasing diagonal. In the center is the inverted triangle shape of the mom, dad and baby. All three groups are connected and the face heights are staggered beautifully. Posing is completely natural; expressions are real and pleasing. Photograph by Frank Frost.

With natural poses, have your antennae up for errant thumbs and hands that will pop up. Always do a perimeter search around each subject to make sure there is nothing unexpected in the posing.

○ POSING LEVELS

Two true experts at posing the midsize to large group are Robert and Suzanne Love. I have witnessed them build groups from other photogra-phers attending one of their workshops and each person, without exception, was amazed when they saw how easy the Loves' technique is and how attractive the arrangement turned out.

The basic principle involved in the Loves technique is the use of different posing levels and the combinations of those levels used adjacent to one another. Here's a brief look at the system:

Level 1, Standing. Each standing subject has his or her weight on their back foot and is posed at a 45-degree angle to the camera, lowering the rear shoulder to diminish overall body size.

Level 2, Tall Kneel. Generally a masculine pose, not unlike a football players' team pose, this pose calls for the man to get down on one knee with his leg bent at 90 degrees. The elbow of the arm on the same side as the knee that is up should rest on the knee.

Level 3, Short Kneel. This is the same pose as above but both knees are on the ground and the person's weight is back on their calves. This pose is good for either men or women, but with women in dresses, they are usually turned at a 45-degree angle.

Level 4, Sitting. The man sits on his buttocks with the leg that is toward the camera curled under the leg that's away from the camera. The elbow rests across his raised knee. Again, for a lady wearing slacks, this is appropriate. However, a seated pose that is more graceful and feminine is when the lady lays on her hip and rolls toward the camera. Her legs then flow out to the side with the ankles crossed. Her top hand can rest on her lower thigh, or in front of her. If she can bring her top knee over to touch the ground, her body produces a beautiful curved line.

Level 5, Lying Down. The man or lady can lay on their side with the hand up to the side of their face, or on their stomach with their arms folded in front of them. This really works better for an individual pose, rather than a group, but it offers another level if needed.

Each face is at a different level and no face is directly below or above another . . .

By intermixing the levels, without defining rows, you can pose ten to twenty people quite easily and informally. Each face is at a different level and no face is directly below or above another,

providing good visual interest. And while the group is really quite highly structured, it doesn't appear that way.

○ STEPLADDERS

A stepladder is a must for large groups and, in fact, should be a permanent tool in your wedding arsenal. Stepladders give you the high angle that lets you fit lots of people together in a tight group, like a bouquet of flowers. Ladders also give you a means to correct low shooting angles, which distort perspective. The tendency is to overuse them, so use a stepladder when you need to or when you want to offer variety in your groups.

A stepladder is the answer to the refrain, "Boy, I sure wish I could get up on that balcony for this shot." Chances are you won't get the opportunity. But one word of caution: have your assistant or someone strong hold the ladder in case the ground gives or you lean the wrong way. Safety first.

In less dramatic ways, a stepladder lets you raise the camera height just slightly so that you can keep the group plane parallel to the film plane for better depth-of-field control.

○ LINKING SHAPES

The bigger the group, the more you must depend on your basic elements of group portrait design—circles, triangles, inverted triangles, diagonals and diamond shapes. You must also really work to highlight and accentuate lines, real and implied, throughout the group. If you lined people up in a row, you would have a very uninteresting "team photo," a concept that is the antithesis of fine group portraiture.

The best way to previsualize this effect is to form subgroups as you start grouping people. For example, how about three bridesmaids here (perhaps forming an inverted triangle), three sisters over on the right (perhaps forming a flowing diagonal line), a brother, a sister and their two kids (perhaps in a diamond shape with the littlest one standing between the mom and the dad). Then

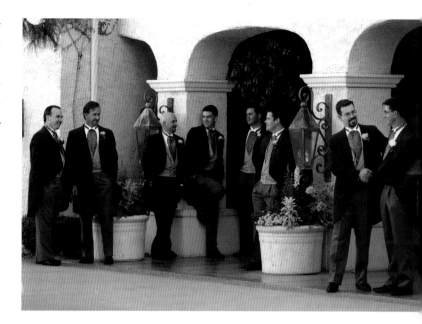

Right: This group breaks all the rules but is still an effective image. It seems casual and unplanned, as if this were a spontaneous event. But look again. The design of the image is wonderful. The arches seem to mirror each individual group and there is a dynamic within each of the three groups. Even though the portrait is a long horizontal line, there are plenty of diagonals and angled lines to offer visual interest. Photograph by Kenneth Sklute. **Bottom:** *Although this is a big group, it's really six small groups all handled well. Entitled, "Wedding in Pleasantville," the idea was born when the photographer knew he would be doing wedding photos at the Cleveland Art Museum. He saw a group of frames in his studio's framing department and thought it would be cute to have the couples in the wedding party "become" art by holding the frames in front of themselves. In the movie,* Pleasantville, *the people who fell in love began to turn from black and white to color. The idea seemed to be perfect. This is an exercise in cohesiveness—making small groups stick together and act as one. Photograph by Robert Kunesh.*

combine the subsets, linking the line of an arm with the line of a dress. Leave a little space between these subgroups, so that the design shapes you've formed don't become too compressed. Let the subgroups flow from one to the next and then analyze the group as a whole to see what you've created.

Remember that arms and hands help complete the composition by creating motion and dynamic lines that can and should lead up into the subjects' faces. Hands and arms can "finish" lines started by the basic shape of the group.

Just because you might form a triangle or a diamond with one subset in a group does not mean that one of the people in that group cannot be used as an integral part of another group. You might find, for example, that the person in the middle of a group of seven unites two diamond shapes. The overlapping circles around these shapes (see diagram on page 76) define each pattern as unique, even though both shapes use the same person. In a portrait like this, each subset could be turned slightly toward center to unify the composition or turned away from center to give a bookend effect.

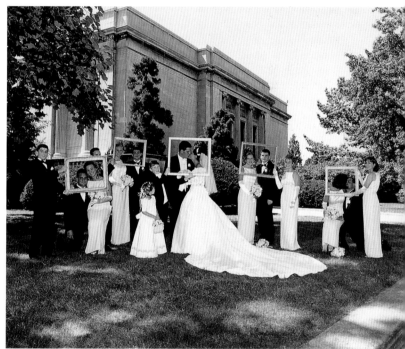

Be aware of intersecting lines that flow through the design. As mentioned earlier, the diagonal is by far the most compelling visual line and can be used repeatedly without fear of overuse. The curving diagonal is even more pleasing and can be mixed with sharper diagonals within the composition.

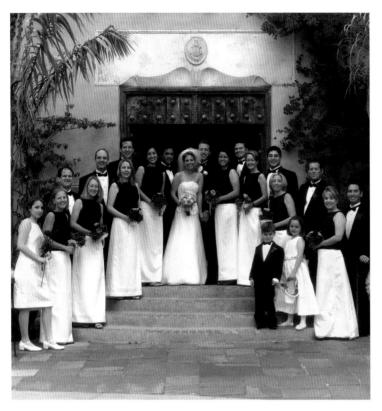

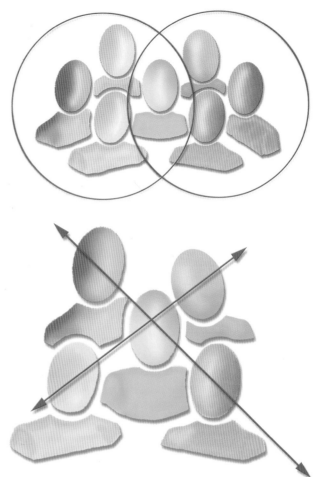

○ THE REALLY BIG GROUP

St. Louis-area photographer David Bentley was asked recently to photograph this huge group (opposite) for Walgreens' in-house magazine. Of the shoot he says, "The only unique thing I did was to put tape on the warehouse floor at the edges of the frame as seen through the lens. Then I asked everyone to please step inside the lines to be in the photo—it saved a lot of time."

Of cautions, Bentley says, "You must be careful where you position the camera for these shots. By this I mean buildings move! Walgreens wanted me on a catwalk, but I could see it sway from the floor. On the third floor where I eventually shot, I had them shut down the conveyor belts and move no forklifts during the exposure."

David used gelled Photogenic strobes and dragged the shutter for one second to build up the ambient light. In other words, the exposure was one second with the strobes firing at the beginning of the exposure. He used Rosco gels and a Polaroid back to match the color of the mercury vapor lights. He kept adding more yellow gel to the strobe heads until he finally got it.

Top Left: The very formal wedding portrait is a difficult image to make. Notice the symmetry to the left and right and the uniformity of the poses of the eight bridesmaids—each elbow is bent at the same place, each bouquet is front and center. The symmetry is contrasted with the curving shapes of the foliage in the background and the flowing lines of the Spanish architecture. Photograph by Kenneth Sklute. Top Right: The overlapping circles around these shapes define each pattern as unique, even though both shapes use the same person. In a portrait like this, each subset could be turned slightly toward center to unify the composition or turned away from center to give a bookend effect. Bottom: Be aware of intersecting lines that flow through the design. As mentioned earlier, the diagonal is by far the most compelling visual line and can be used repeatedly without fear of overuse. Diagram concepts courtesy of Norman Phillips.

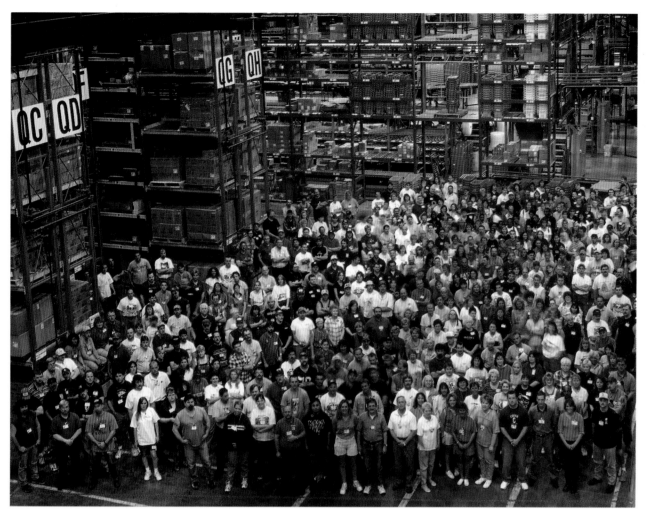

David Bentley photographed this huge, impossibly large group by dragging the shutter for one second to build up the ambient light of the warehouse, and firing catwalk-mounted strobes, gelled to match the mercury-vapor lights. Bentley taped off the floor beforehand so he could see the outer perimeter of his composition. The client, Walgreens, wanted to show not only the employees, but the warehouse in which they work. Although a few people moved during the one-second exposure, the majority are still and looking directly at the camera. By the way, the client was delighted with the result.

As you can see by the final group shot that was used for the Walgreens' magazine, there are a few people that moved during the one-second exposure, but most are sharp and most are looking directly at the camera. This is really the best one can hope for with this kind of group.

For really big groups like this one, have the subjects stand close together, touching. This minimizes the space between people, allowing you to get a larger head size for each person. One directive you must give to the group is that they must be able to see the camera with both eyes. This will ensure that you see all of their faces and that none will be hiding behind the person in front of them.

With big groups, fight the tendency to "line 'em up and shoot 'em." This is, after all, a portrait and not a team photo. You can incorporate all types of design elements into even the largest groups.

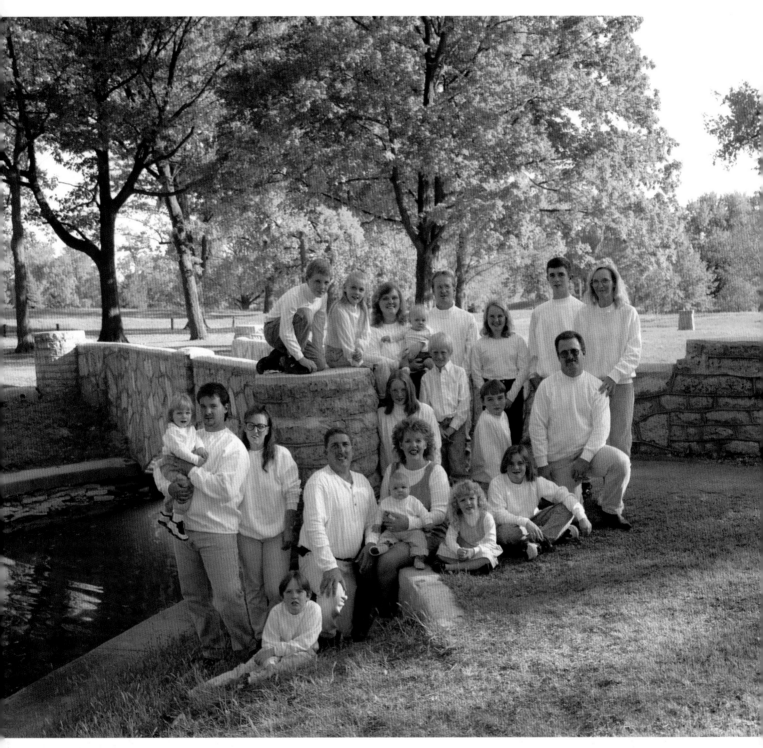

Above: Beautiful light and a beautiful day highlight this portrait of twenty-one. If you look closely, you will see a Z-shaped pattern running throughout the grouping. The picture uses found levels to give the group dynamics and height, and even though some of the kids are squirming, it's still a memorable family portrait. This portrait also demonstrates the importance of matching clothing colors. Photograph by Michael Ayers. **Opposite:** If the average photographer had tried to find a blue stone that matched the bridesmaids' dresses and groomsmen's vests, he undoubtedly would have been looking for a long time. Not so for this lucky photographer. The color coordination with the steps and buildings is near perfect. Although this group has great structure—two sweeping diagonals intersecting the square format—there is great casualness and joy in the poses. The bride and groom certainly stand out, being the tallest figures in the frame. Photograph by Anthony Cava.

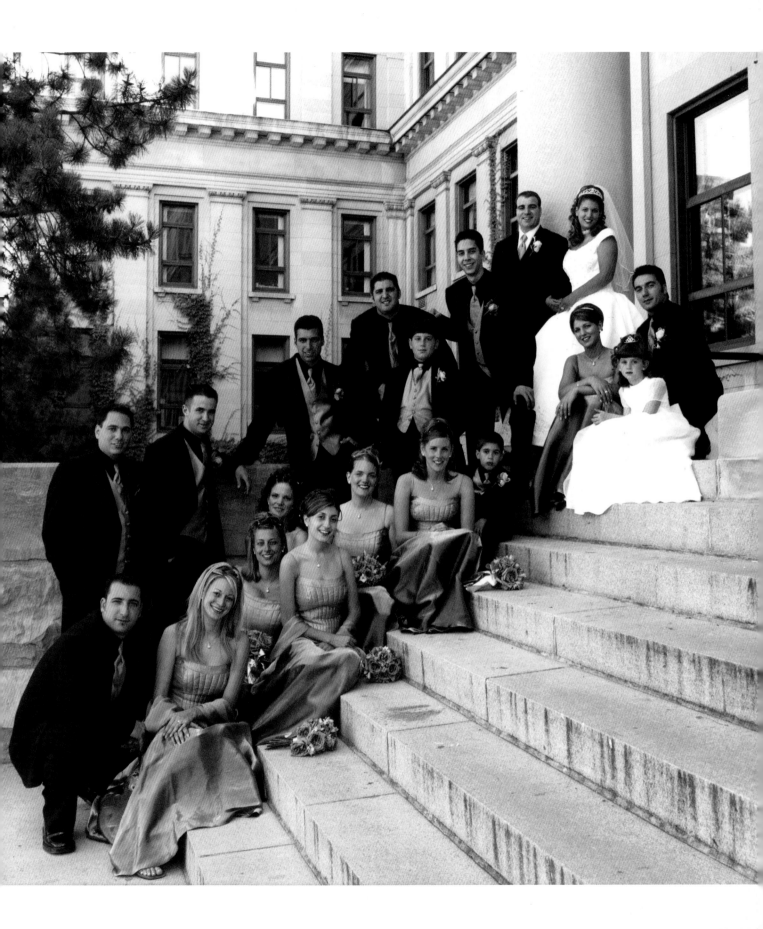

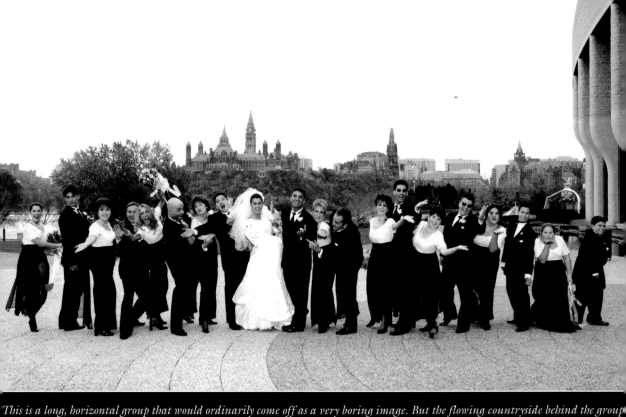

This is a long, horizontal group that would ordinarily come off as a very boring image. But the flowing countryside behind the group and the concentric circles seen in the foreground stone serve to break up the long static horizontal. When you look at this pose you realize the photographer must've had complete control of this group to get them to do this. Photograph by Anthony Cava.

5

OUTDOOR LIGHTING

Groups may be photographed in open sunlight or open shade. They may be backlit, sidelit or frontlit. What is more important than the direction of the light is the evenness of the light. As Robert Love says, the secret to a great group portrait is to "light them evenly from left to right and from front to back." Good outdoor lighting is primarily what separates the good group photographers from the great ones. Learning to control, predict and alter daylight to suit the needs of the group to be photographed is the ultimate objective of the group portrait photographer.

○ ROUNDNESS

The human face consists of a series of planes, very few of which are completely flat. The human face is sculpted and round. It is the job of a portrait photographer to show the contours of the human face. This is done primarily with highlights and shadows. Highlights are areas that are illuminated by the main light source; shadows are areas that are not. The interplay of highlight and shadow creates roundness and shows form. Just as a sculptor models clay to create the illusion of form, so light models the shape of the face to give it depth and roundness.

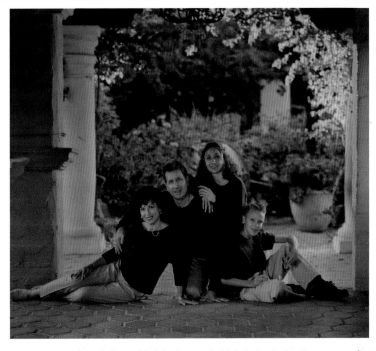

One might take a look at this location and think it is absolutely perfect. It provides soft late afternoon sidelight that models and shapes faces, it has a near-perfect background of multicolored flowers and architecture that has its own light, and it has beautiful California mission architecture. The lighting is basic backlighting with fill-in from diffused sidelight and bounce off of the adobe-colored columns. Photograph by Heidi Mauracher.

The term is used to describe the difference in intensity between the shadow and highlight side of the face. It is expressed numerically—3:1, for example, which means that the highlight side of the face is three times brighter than the shadow side.

Ratios are useful because they determine how much local contrast there will be in the portrait. They do not determine the overall contrast of the scene; rather, lighting ratios determine how much contrast you will give to the lighting of the group.

Note: In the descriptions that follow, the key light refers to the main light source. The fill light is the source of illumination that fills in the shadows created by the main or key light. In outdoor lighting situations, the key light can either be daylight or artificial light, such as that from an electronic flash or reflector. The fill light outdoors can also be either daylight or flash.

Since lighting ratios reflect the difference in intensity between the fill light and the key light, the ratio is an indication of how much shadow detail you will have in the final portrait. Since the fill light controls the degree to which the shadows are illuminated, it is important to keep the lighting ratio fairly constant. A desirable ratio for outdoor group portraits in color is 3:1 because of the rather limited tonal range of color printing papers.

A 2:1 ratio is the lowest lighting ratio you should employ. It shows only minimal roundness in the face and is most desirable for high key effects. High key portraits are those with low lighting ratios, light tones, and usually a light background. In a 2:1 lighting ratio the key and fill light sources are the same intensity.

A 3:1 lighting ratio is produced when the key light is one stop greater in intensity than the fill light. Here's how the ratio is determined: one unit of light on both sides of the face from the fill light, and two units of light on the highlight side from the key light; thus a 3:1 ratio. This ratio is the most preferred for color and black & white because it will yield an exposure with excellent

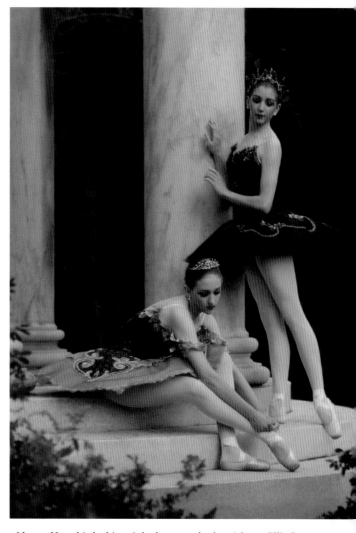

Above: You think this might be open shade with no fill? Guess again. The photo was taken in late evening as the sun disappeared behind the trees. The sky over and in front of the ballerinas was open sky, which created a very soft, beautiful lighting. The photographer used a small amount of on-camera fill-flash to soften the shadows. The image was made with a Hasselblad with 180mm lens, and Kodak PPF 400 film exposed for 1/30 at f/5.6. The lighting ratio is a gorgeous 3:1. Photograph by Dale Hansen. *Opposite:* Beautiful natural daylight with no fill-in source. The backlight gives dimension to the background and also with the faces in true profile, there is just enough of a highlight on the girl's face to define a lighting pattern. The photographer wanted to isolate the moment of a tender kiss and a touch. Note that the portrait is made more romantic by their lips being close together, but not touching. A Mamiya RB 67 camera and 250mm lens were used to make the shot. Kodak PPF 400 film was exposed for 1/60 at f/8. The ratio is a hard 3:1. Photograph by Bill Duncan.

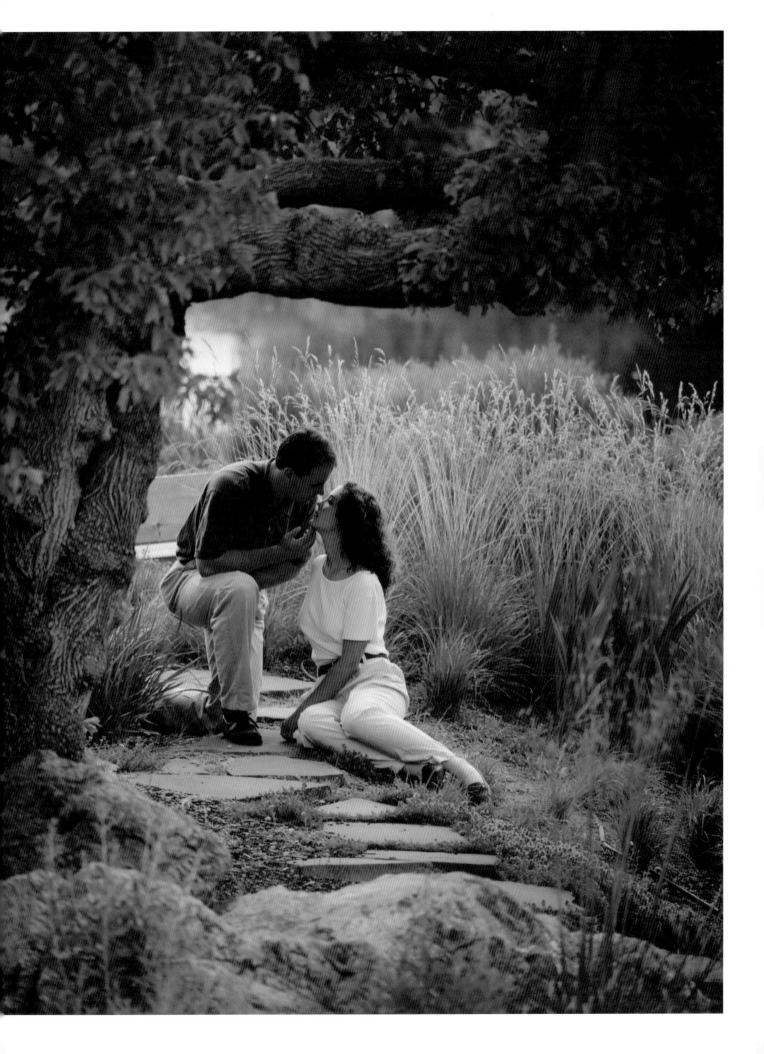

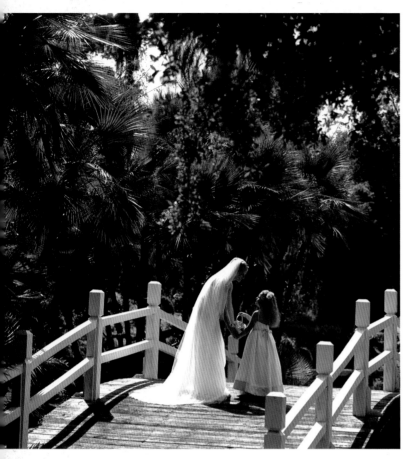

Finding good light and finding a great location are sometimes mutually exclusive. Here, the photographer found both. The white of the dresses and the natural reflectance of the board-walk bridge provide all the fill-in illumination that is needed for a perfect 3:1 lighting ratio outdoors. The backlight rims the bride and little girl perfectly, defining delicate shapes and textures. The composition is such that the bridge and overhanging palms all lead your eye to this lovely couple. Photograph by Rick Ferro.

shadow and highlight detail. It shows good roundness in the face and is ideal for rendering average-shaped faces.

A 4:1 ratio (the key light is two stops greater in intensity than the fill light) is used when a slimming or dramatic effect is desired. In a 4:1 ratio, the shadow side of the face loses its slight glow and the accent of the portrait becomes the highlights. Ratios of 4:1 and higher are considered low key portraits. Low key portraits are characterized by a higher lighting ratio, dark tones and usually a dark background.

A 5:1 ratio (the key light is three stops greater than the fill light) and higher is considered almost a high-contrast rendition. It is ideal for conveying a dramatic effect to your subject and is often used in character studies. Shadow detail is minimal at the higher ratios and as a result, they are not recommended for color films unless your only concern is highlight detail.

○ FINDING GOOD LIGHT

Unlike the studio, where you can set the lights to obtain any effect you want, in nature you must use the light that you find. By far the best place to make outdoor group portraits is in the shade, away from direct sunlight.

Shade is nothing more than diffused sunlight. Contrary to popular belief, shade is not directionless. It has a definite direction. The best shade for groups is found in or near a clearing in the woods. Where trees provide an overhang above the subjects, the light is blocked. In a clearing, diffused light filters in from the sides, producing better modeling on the face than in open shade.

Open shade is overhead in nature and most unflattering. Like noontime sun, it leaves deep shadows in the eye sockets and under the nose and chin of the subjects. The best kind of shade comes from an angle. If forced to shoot your group in open shade, you must fill-in the daylight with a frontal flash or reflector.

Another popular misconception about shade is that it is always a soft light. Particularly on overcast days, shade can be harsh, producing bright highlights and deep shadows, especially around midday. Move under an overhang, such as a tree with low-hanging branches or a covered porch, and you will immediately notice that the light is less harsh and that it also has good direction. The quality of light will also be less overhead in nature—coming from the side, not obscured by the overhang.

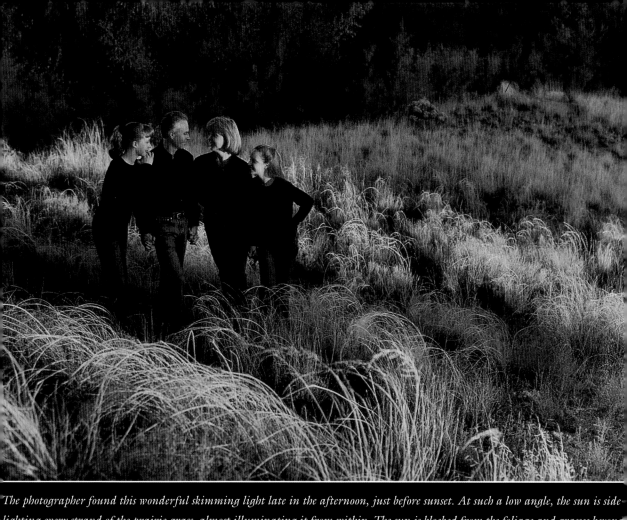

The photographer found this wonderful skimming light late in the afternoon, just before sunset. At such a low angle, the sun is side-lighting every strand of the prairie grass, almost illuminating it from within. The sun is blocked from the foliage and grasses beyond the subjects, making the area subdued so that the subjects stand out. There is no source of fill-in used, only the minimal wraparound light of the sun on the subjects, which makes the black and blue tones of the subjects' clothing even more prominent in the sunlit scene. One trick in environmental portraiture is to limit the amount of sky and horizon in the image. By minimizing the sky, the subjects become more prominent. Here, a high vantage point eliminates any sky or horizon line from the image. Photograph by Frank Frost.

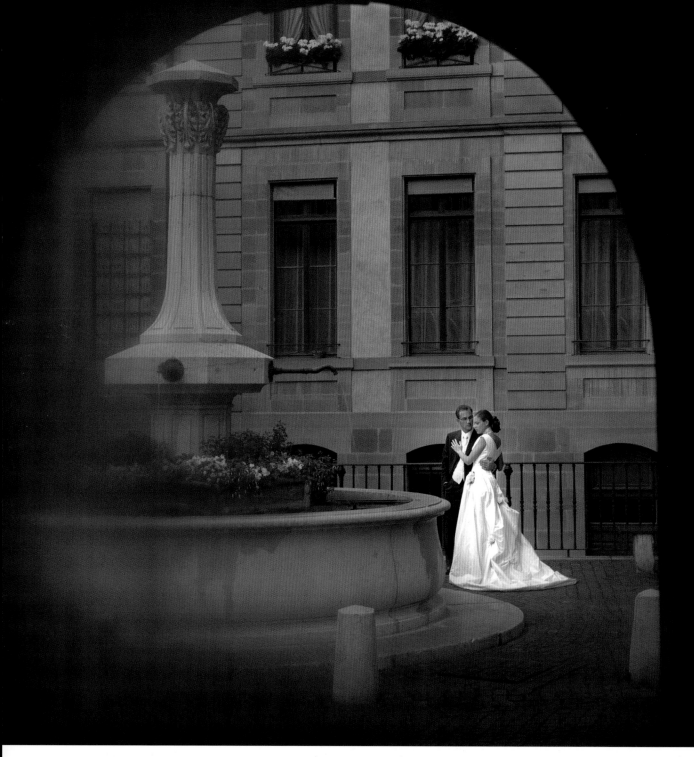

Above: *Open shade in an open courtyard can be completely overhead in nature, but in this case the light is so diffuse as to be coming from everywhere. There is only slight frontal direction to the light and almost no shadows at all. The black foreground arch and the darkened and diffused stonework and fountain all serve to focus your eye on the bride and groom. Photograph by Vladimir Bekker.* ***Opposite:*** *This is an image made at twilight. You can see the last rays of the sun on the mountaintops in the background. Since the sun is behind and to the left, there is a gentle backlighting, rimming the hair of the subjects in the group. The open sky is now the key light and it is soft and flattering. This photographer rarely uses any source of fill-in light for his outdoor group portraits, preferring instead the natural softbox that is the sky at twilight. Photograph by Frank Frost.*

THE BEST LIGHT

As many of the great photographs in this book illustrate, the best time of day for making great group pictures is just after the sun has set. The sky becomes a huge softbox and the effect of the lighting on your subjects is soft and even, with no harsh shadows.

There are two problems with working with this great light. One, it's dim. You will need to use medium to fast films combined with slow shutter speeds, which can be problematic if there are children being posed. Working in subdued light also restricts your depth of field by virtue of having to choose wide apertures. The second problem in working with this light is that twilight does not produce catchlights, white specular highlights, in the eyes of the subjects. For this reason, most photographers augment the twilight with some type of flash, either barebulb flash or softbox-mounted flash that provides a twinkle in the eye.

ONE MAIN LIGHT

Just as in the studio, it is important to have only one main light in your groups. This is a fundamental in portraiture. Other lights can modify the main light, but, just as in nature, there should be a single main light source. Most photographers who shoot a lot of group portraits subscribe to the use of a single main light for groups, indoors or out, and filling the shadows of the main light with one or more flash units.

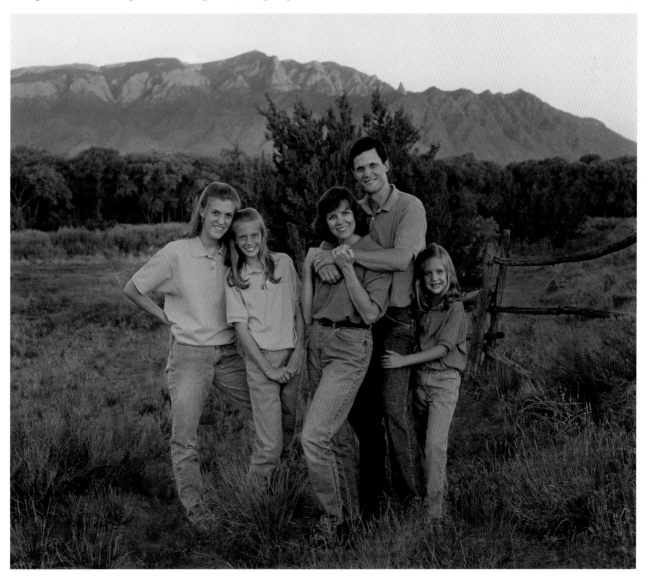

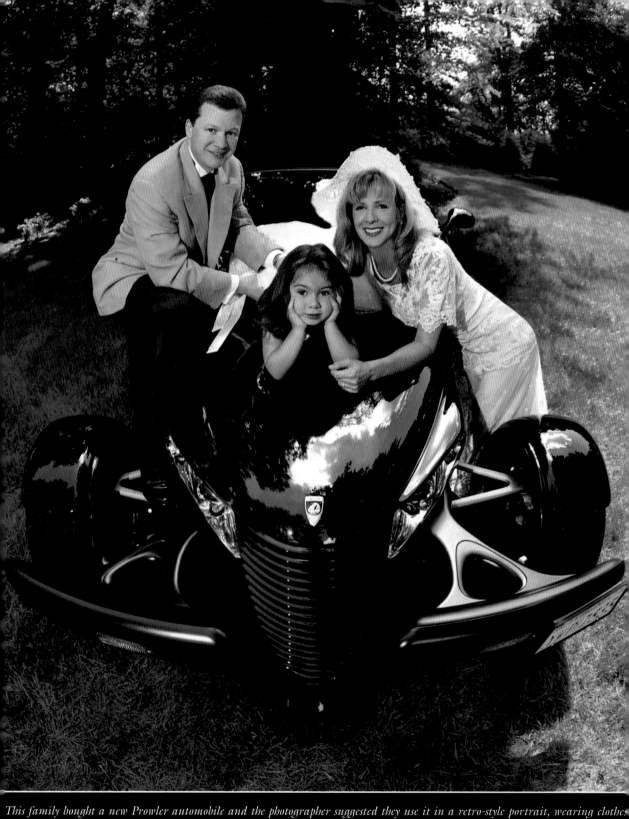

This family bought a new Prowler automobile and the photographer suggested they use it in a retro-style portrait, wearing clothes that looked a little like '30s fashions. The portrait was made on a hill with the Prowler angled toward the photographer, who stood on a six-foot stepladder looking down on the subjects. The scene was backlighted, with the ambient light and the barebulb flash read-

○ REFLECTORS

You are at the mercy of nature when you are looking for a lighting location. Sometimes it is difficult to find the right type of light for your needs. It is a good idea to carry along a portable light reflector. The size of the reflector should be fairly large—the larger it is the more effective it will be. Portable light discs, which are reflectors made of fabric mounted on a flexible and collapsible circular or rectangular frame, come in a variety of diameters and are a very effective means of fill-in illumination. They are available from a number of manufacturers and come in silver (for maximum fill output), white, gold foil (for a warming fill light), and black (for subtractive effects).

When the shadows produced by diffused light are harsh and deep, or even when you just want to add a little sparkle to the eyes of your subjects, use a large reflector or even several reflectors. It helps to have an assistant or several light stands with clamps so that you can precisely set the reflectors. Be sure to position them outside the frame. With foil-type reflectors used close to the subject, you can even sometimes overpower the ambient light, creating a pleasing and flattering lighting pattern.

Reflectors should be used close to the subject, just out of view of the camera lens. You will have to adjust it several times to create the right amount of fill-in. Always observe lighting effects from the camera position. Be careful about bouncing light in from beneath your subjects. Lighting coming from under the eye/nose axis is generally unflattering. Try to "focus" your reflectors (this really requires an assistant), so that you are only filling the shadows that need filling in.

○ FILL-IN FLASH

A more predictable form of fill-in is electronic flash. As mentioned, many photographers shooting groups use barebulb flash, a portable flash unit with a vertical flash tube, like a beacon, that fires the flash a full 360 degrees with the reflector removed. You can use as wide a lens as you own

and you won't get flash falloff with barebulb flash. Barebulb flash produces a sharp, sparkly light, which is too harsh for almost every type of photography except outdoor groups. The trick is not to overpower the daylight. This is the best source of even fill-in illumination. Look at the environmental portraits by Bill McIntosh, which are sprinkled throughout this book. In each of his outdoor portraits he uses barebulb flash to either fill-in backlit subjects or to add a little punch to sunlit subjects when the sun is very low, early in the morning or at sunset.

Other photographers like to soften their fill-flash. Robert Love, for example, uses a Lumedyne strobe inside of a 24-inch softbox. He triggers the strobe cordlessly with a radio remote control. Instead of using the fill-in flash head on or at a

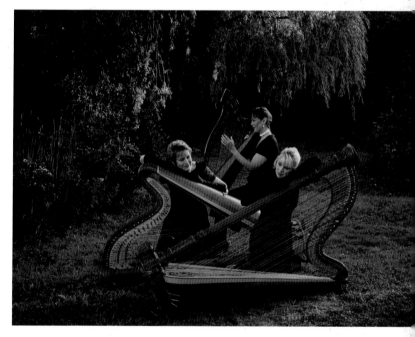

This gorgeous composition, called "Harp to Harp," consists of a series of overlapping triangles. Every prominent detail is visible in the photograph, thanks to the careful control of the lighting. To create this image, the women and the harps were softly backlit, as was the foliage in the background. A diffused Metz flash was used at the camera position at about 1½ stops less output than the ambient light—just enough to fill in the faces and give a little sparkle to the beautiful wood of the harps, but not enough to bring out any detail in the black clothing. Photograph by Patrick Rice.

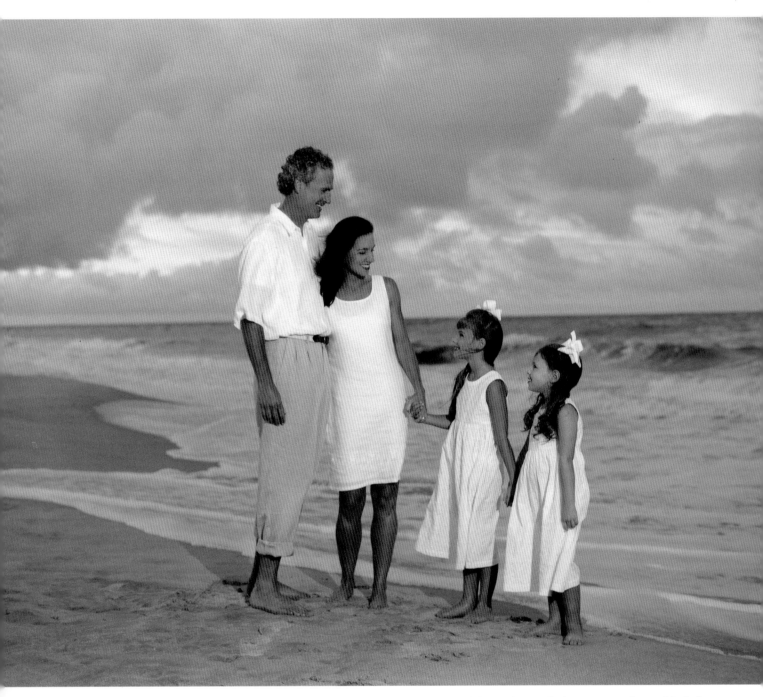

The sky on the oceanfront just after the sun goes down is very dramatic. The light on the family, however, was flat and lacked contrast. The photographer used a Lumedyne barebulb strobe close to the camera position to make the people stand out. The exposure for the sky was ⅛ at f/8. To get more saturation in the sky, the photographer set the strobe output for f/8 and the shutter for 1/60, thereby underexposing the sky by one f-stop. By underexposing the ambient light by one stop, the flash became the key light and, while it made the sky much deeper, it also created a set of shadows from the flash. In this case, the resulting shadows are not objectionable. A Mamiya RZ 67 with 90mm lens and NHG II 800 film were used to create the image. Photograph by Bill McIntosh.

slight angle, he often uses his flash at a 45-degree angle to his subjects (for small groups) for a modeled fill-in. For larger groups he uses the softbox next to the camera for more even coverage.

Other photographers, especially those shooting 35mm systems, prefer on-camera TTL flash. Many on-camera TTL flash systems use a mode for TTL fill-in flash that will balance the flash output to the ambient-light exposure for balanced fill-flash. Many such systems are also controllable by virtue of flash-output compensation that allows you to dial in full- or fractional-stop output changes for the desired ratio of ambient-to-fill illumination. They are marvelous systems and, of more importance, they are reliable and predictable. Some of these systems also allow you to remove the flash from the camera with a TTL remote cord.

○ Using Flash-Fill, Metering and Exposure

Here is the scenario for measuring and setting the light output for a fill-in flash situation. This will produce a true fill light with the ambient light stronger than the fill-in light.

First meter the scene. It is best to use a hand-held incident meter, with the hemisphere pointed at the camera from the group position. In this hypothetical example, the metered exposure is $\frac{1}{15}$ at f/8. Now, with a flash meter, meter the flash only. Your goal is for the output to be one stop less than the ambient exposure. Adjust flash output or flash-to-subject distance until your flash reading is f/5.6. Set the camera to $\frac{1}{15}$ at f/8. If using medium format, a Polaroid test print is a good idea.

If the light is dropping or the sky is brilliant in the scene and you want to shoot for optimal color saturation in the background, overpower the daylight with flash. Returning to the hypothetical situation where the daylight exposure was $\frac{1}{15}$ at f/8, now adjust your flash output so your flash meter reading is f/11, a stop more powerful than the daylight. Set your camera to $\frac{1}{15}$ at f/11. The flash is now the key light and the soft twilight is the fill light. The problem with this is that you will get a

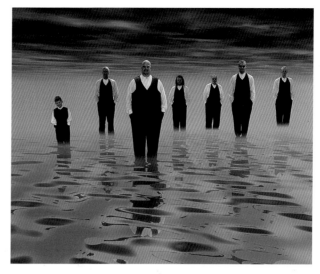

This highly unusual group shot was created for competition. All the groomsmen were shot individually, head-on and back-lighted with moderate fill. Then each of the images was brought into the scene created in Bryce 3D®, a 3-D image-editing program, and Adobe Photoshop. The individuals were "sunk" and scaled correctly and the shadows created on the rippling water. The unworldly sky was a final effect. Notice that even though the individuals are separated and different sizes, there are still group dynamics at work. Photograph by Richard Pahl.

separate set of shadows from the flash. This can be OK, however, since there aren't really any shadows from the twilight. Keep in mind that it is one of the side effects.

Remember that electronic flash falls off in intensity rather quickly, so be sure to take your meter readings from the center of your group and even from either end to be on the safe side. With a small group of three or four you can get away with moving the strobe away from the camera to get better modeling, but not with larger groups, as the falloff is too great. You can, however, add a second flash of equal intensity and distance on the opposite side of the camera to help widen the light.

It is also important to remember that you are balancing two light sources in one scene. The ambient light exposure will dictate the exposure on the background and the subjects. The flash exposure only affects the subjects. When you hear of photographers "dragging the shutter" it refers

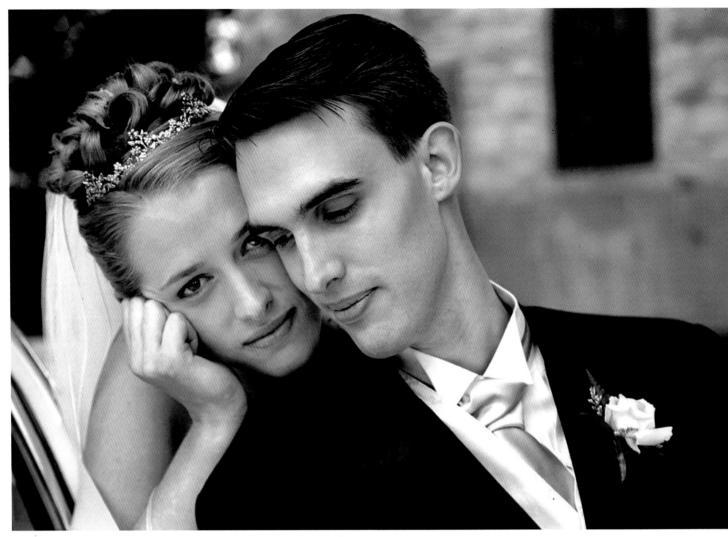

Above: This image was made by available daylight. Some of the fill is achieved by light bouncing around from the automobile. What is amazing about this image is that diffused daylight rarely produces such elegant highlight brilliance. Note too that the background is blown out but the figures are completely sharp from the tip of the groom's nose to the back of his ear. The pose has great direction and sophistication, too. Photograph by David Anthony Williams. Opposite: This elegant portrait is a study in triangles—they are found in the group itself, in the incoming surf and the silhouetted, jutting coastline. The lighting used was direct diffused skylight. Though the sun was setting, the light from the sky was frontal in nature. All the photographer had to do was face the group toward the light and she got perfect modeling. The sky portion of the image was given a dark orange color and the water itself was brightened in Photoshop. Photograph by Heidi Mauracher.

to using a shutter speed slower than X sync speed in order to expose the background properly. Understanding this concept is the essence of flash-fill.

○ BACKGROUND CONTROL

The best type of background for a portrait made in the shade is monochromatic. If the background is all the same color, the subjects will stand out from it. Problems arise when there are patches of sunlight in the background. These light patches can be minimized by shooting at wide lens apertures. The shallow depth of field blurs the background so that light and dark tones merge. You can also use a diffuser over the camera lens to give your portrait an overall misty feeling. You will also be minimizing a distracting background.

Another way to minimize a distracting background is in printing. By burning-in or diffusing the background you make it darker, softer or otherwise less noticeable. This technique is really simple in Photoshop, since it's fairly easy to select the subjects, invert the selection so that the background is selected, and perform all sorts of maneuvers on it, from diffusion to color correction to density correction.

Some photographers, when working outdoors, prefer to place more space between group members to allow the background to become more integrated into the overall design of the image.

○ DIRECT SUNLIGHT

Sometimes you are forced to photograph your groups in bright sunlight. While not the best scenario, it is still possible. Turn your group so the direct sunlight is backlighting or rimlighting the group. Backlighting voids the harshness of the light and prevents your subjects from squinting. Of course, you need to fill in the backlight with strobe (reflectors would cause your subjects to squint) and you also need to be careful not to underexpose in backlit situations. It is best to give

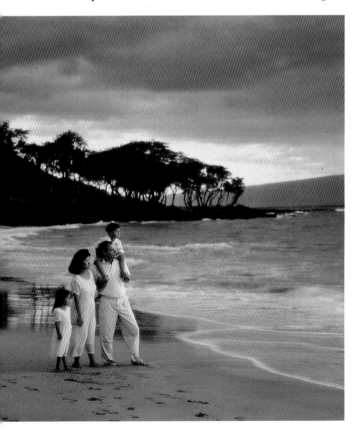

your exposure another third to half stop of exposure in backlit portraits in order to open up the skin tones.

Don't trust your in-camera meter in backlit situations. It will read the bright background and highlights on the hair instead of the exposure on the faces. If you expose for the background light intensity, you will silhouette the subjects. If you have no other meter than the in-camera one, move in close and take a close-up reading on your subjects. It is really best to use a handheld incident meter in backlit situations. Be sure, however, to shield the hemisphere from direct backlight when taking a reading for the faces.

If the sun is low in the sky, you can use crosslighting (split lighting) to get good modeling on your group. Almost half of the face will be in shadow while the other half is highlighted. You must be careful to position subjects so that the sun's side-lighting does not hollow out the eye sockets on the highlight side of the face. You must also position your subjects so that one person's head doesn't block the light of the person next to him or her. There must adequate fill-in from the shadow side of camera so that the shadows don't go dead. Try to keep your fill-in flash output equal to or about a stop less than your daylight exposure.

It is important to check the background while composing a portrait in direct sunlight. Since there is considerably more light than in a portrait made in the shade, the tendency is to use an average shutter speed like $\frac{1}{250}$ with a smaller-than-usual aperture like f/11. Smaller apertures will sharpen up the background and distract from your subject. Preview the depth of field to analyze the background. Use a faster shutter speed and wider lens aperture to minimize background effects in these situations.

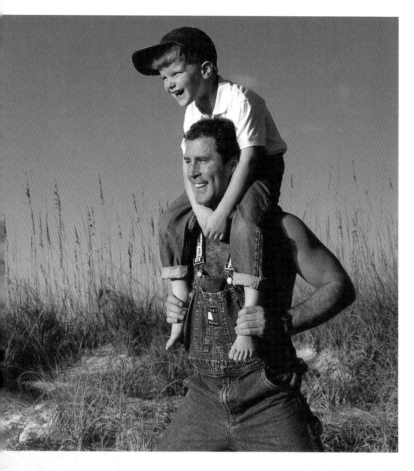

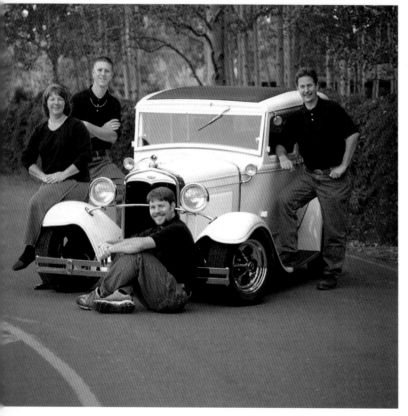

Left: Direct sunlight can often be a formula for disaster, but not here. Subjects are rarely seen looking directly into the sun, but since it is sunrise and the sun is very low, the photographer has them look just to the left of the bright light. Notice the great roundness caused by the skimming angle of the light. As you can see, no fill but the sandy beach was used. Photograph by Monte Zucker. *Bottom:* The hot rod is the family's most prized possession. The photographer found a good location and photographed the scene in late afternoon light. The golden light of sunset is highlighting the fall foliage in the out-of-focus background. The skylight acts like a huge softbox—notice the long, elegant highlights on the car's reflective surfaces. This light is also good for modeling the faces. Excellent attire coordination is the finishing touch to this lasting portrait. Photograph by Robert Love.

○ PROBLEMS OUTDOORS

One thing you must watch for outdoors is subject separation from the background. A dark-haired group against a dark green forest background will not separate tonally, creating a tonal merger. Controlling the amount of flash fill or increasing the background exposure would be logical solutions to the problem.

Natural subject positioning is sometimes a problem when working outdoors. If possible, a fence makes a good subject support. If you have to pose the group on the ground, be sure it is not wet or muddy. Bring along a small blanket, which, when folded, can be hidden beneath the subjects. It will ease the discomfort of a long session and also keep the subjects clean and dry.

If possible, always shoot with a tripod. Shutter speeds will generally be on the slow side, especially when shooting in shade. Also, a tripod helps you compose more carefully, and gives you the freedom to walk around the scene and adjust things as well as to converse freely with your subjects.

Sometimes you may choose a beautiful location for a portrait, but the background is totally unworkable. It may be a bald sky or a cluttered background. The best way to handle such backgrounds is with a soft-focus filter or vignette. The soft-focus filter lowers the overall contrast of the scene and background, and fill flash can then be

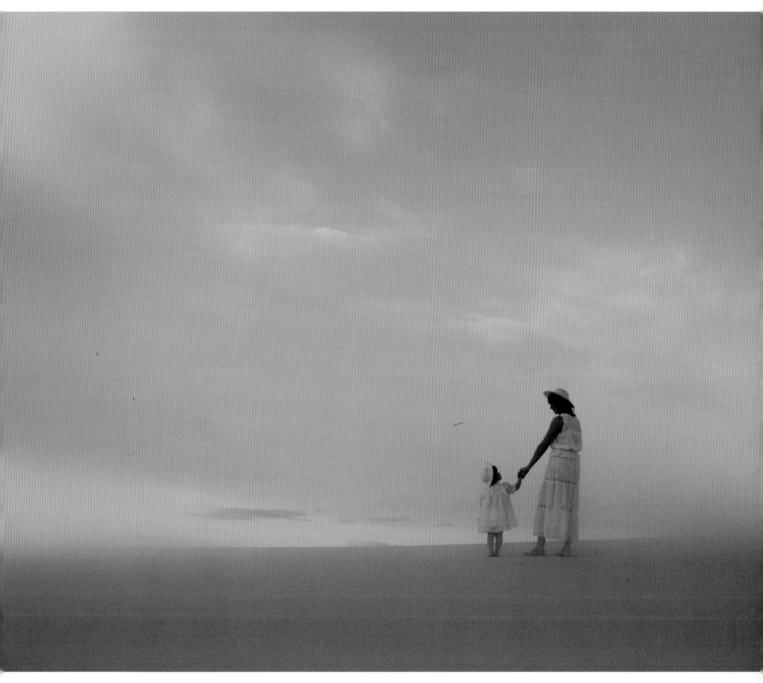

This elegant shot of mother and daughter was given an ethereal feeling by the addition of atmospheric fog in Photoshop. The original image was made at twilight with no fill-in light, so the posing had to be perfect, since the forms rather than the surface texture and details were what was most important. Perfect placement in the frame and the diffusion and fog effects make the picture look like a fond memory. Photograph by Gary Fagan.

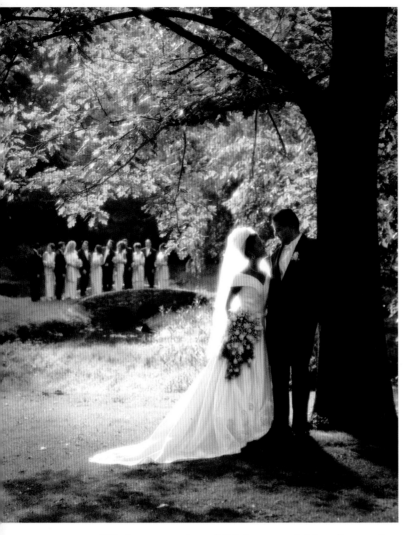

This is a masterpiece of lighting control. Most photographers would not even attempt this shot. The bride and groom were in near silhouette and the wedding party, way off in the background, was also backlit. A minimal amount of fill-in flash was used in the foreground—not enough to brighten faces, but enough to record detail in the dress and bouquet. The photographer wanted the rim- and backlighting to predominate. Photograph by Kenneth Sklute.

used to raise the light level on the subjects. The vignette masks out unwanted areas of the background or foreground. Vignettes are black or white opaque or transparent cards held in an adjustable lens stage that can be racked in and out for the desired effect. Since the vignette is so close to the lens, it is automatically out of focus unless you are stopped down to an intermediate or small f-stop.

Another problem you may encounter is excess cool coloration in portraits taken in shade. If your subject is standing in a grove of trees surrounded by green foliage, there is a good chance green will be reflected into the group. If the subject is exposed to clear, blue, open sky, there may be an excess of cyan in the skin tones. This won't affect your black & white shots, but when working in color, you should beware.

In order to correct green or cyan coloration, you must first observe it. While you are setting up, your eyes will become accustomed to seeing the off-color rendering. Color film is not as forgiving. Study the faces carefully and especially note the coloration of the shadow areas of the face. If the color of the light is neutral, you will see gray in the shadows. If not, you will see either green or cyan.

To correct this coloration, use color compensating (CC) filters over the lens. These are usually gelatin filters that fit in a gel filter holder. To correct for excess green coloration, use a CC 10M (magenta) or CC 15M filter. To correct for a cyan coloration, use a CC 10R (red) or CC 15R filter. This should neutralize the color shift in your scene. Alternately, you can use warming filters, of which there are quite a few. These will generally correct the coolness of shade scenes. Also, fill flash will often wipe out the color shift in the shadows, particularly if the flash output matches or is close to the ambient light exposure.

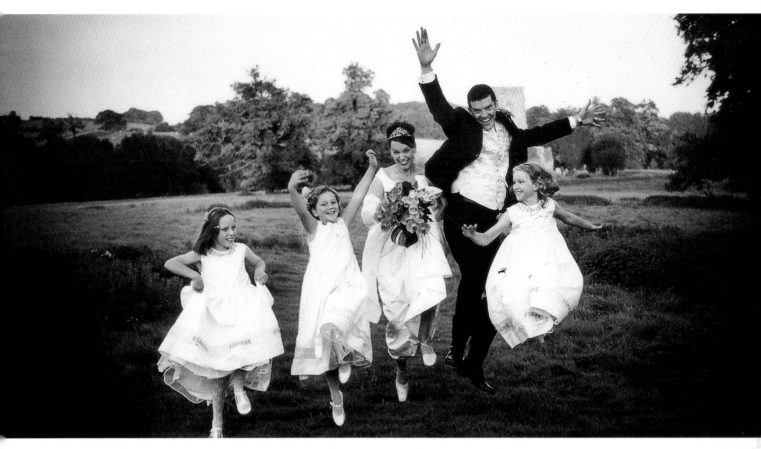

This is a type of group portrait that is popular in England. There is no telling how many takes this required, but the jumping action of the group is perfect. The countryside is an elegant background that contrasts the "playground" pose. The photographer needed enough light and fast enough film to create a very short shutter speed to completely stop the action. He then darkened the frame edges and cropped the image to highlight the joy of this wonderful family. Photograph by Stephen Pugh.

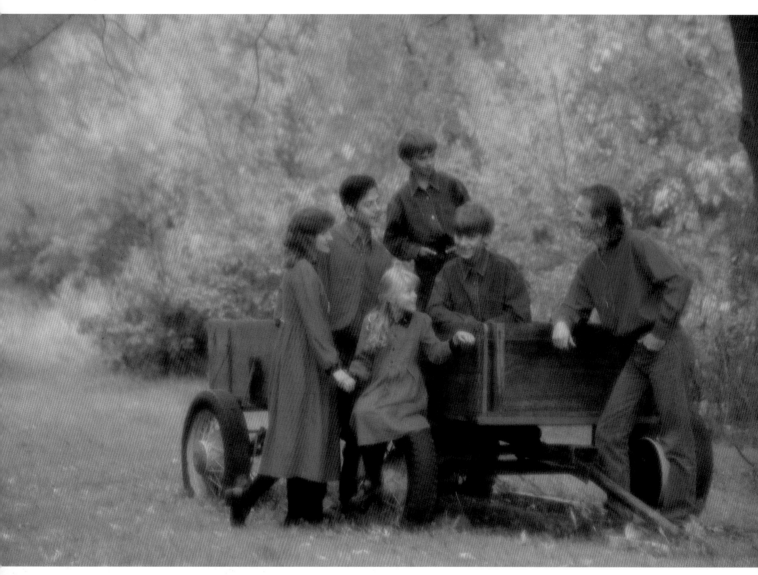

Golden afternoon light and on-camera diffusion with fast film helped define this fun-to-look-at outdoor portrait. The photographer used a diffused flash to fill in the backlighting. The posing is terrific here—notice the central diamond shape of the four kids, bracketed by the mom and dad, who are both leaning in. The family is tied together either by touch or by the direction in which they are gazing. Notice the two boys at the top of the composition and the blond daughter are staring at their dad but the lower boy is gazing back at his sister, creating a flawless composition within the overall composition. The expressions are priceless, as is the color coordination of all six outfits. Photograph by Robert Love.

This portrait could very easily be a painting. The composition is superb—a simple diagonal line. On-camera diffusion, fast film and generous backlighting with minimal flash fill make this photo an unforgettable family portrait. The dog owner, positioned just to the right of the camera, held the dog's attention during the moment of exposure. The photographer chose backlighting to edge light the shape and hair of all three subjects, lending drama and impact to the image. The background completely lacks distracting elements so that the three subjects are predominant. The feeling of bright sunlight adds to the innocence and texture of the image. This is the type of image that would be a hallmark in a family's treasured memories. Photograph by Robert Love.

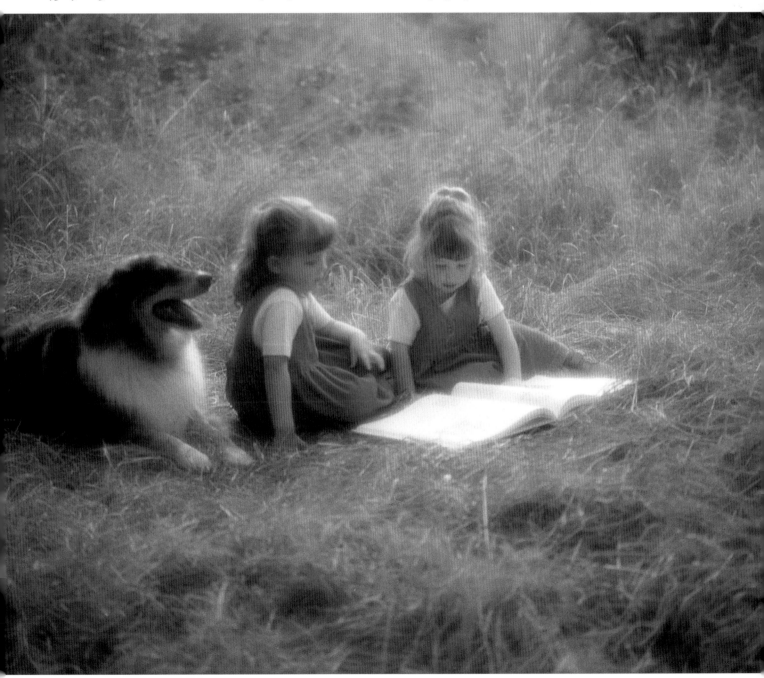

6

INDOOR LIGHTING

The various complexities of lighting in the studio are not really factors when we talk about lighting groups indoors. The key is always to light the subjects evenly from left to right and from front to back. There cannot be any "holes" in the lighting and this is particularly difficult with large groups.

It is irrelevant to talk about portrait lighting patterns here (like paramount, loop and Rembrandt lighting). Instead, you should be concerned about getting the lights high enough to model the subjects' faces and getting the light off to the side so that it is not a flat frontal lighting. But again, these aspects of the lighting are dictated by the size of the group and the area in which you must photograph them. What is important is that you create a one-light look, as you'd find in nature. Various sources of fill light will be discussed throughout, but in every instance, one should strive for a single main-light look in indoor lighting.

○ FEATHERING

Feathering means using the edge, rather than the hot core, of the light source. If you aim a light source directly at your group, you will find that

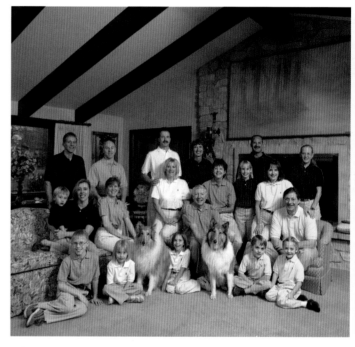

This is a handsome family portrait of an extended family. All the individual families are dressed in differently colored shirts. The photographer used umbrellas to light both the group and the room. The main light was set up to the right of the camera and feathered across the group to light them evenly. A fill umbrella was used on the opposite side of the camera to fill in the shadows and to light the cavernous room. Photograph by Michael Ayers.

while the strobe's modeling light might trick you into thinking the lighting is even, it is really falling off at the ends of the group. Feathering will help to light your group more evenly because you are aiming the light source past the group, using the edge of the light.

Feathering can be done with umbrellas or undiffused lights by aiming the light past the group so that you are only using the edge of the light. It might call for aiming the light up and over the group, using just the edge of the light to light each of the subjects. However, since you are using the edge of the light, you will sometimes cause the level of light to drop off. Always check the results in the viewfinder and with a meter.

Another trick is to move the light source back so that it is less intense overall, but covers a wider area. The light will be harsher and less diffused the farther you move it back.

○ Lighting the Large Room or Dance Floor

Feathering is the technique used to light large areas like the dance floor of a wedding reception. Umbrella lights are set up on stands, which are taped securely to the floor. The umbrellas are focused to attain maximum light output (see photo on page 102). Usually the umbrellas are positioned in the corners of the room and feathered up and out so their core of light is pointed past the center of the room, and will spread evenly across the room. All of the umbrellas are slaved (with either radio or optical slaves) so that when the photographer triggers his or her flash (either on-camera or off-camera flash), all of the umbrellas will fire in sync. The effect is beautiful, allowing the photographer to shoot anyone anywhere on the dance floor without having to set up the lighting for each shot.

Another way to light the dance floor is to use quartz-halogen lights on stands positioned throughout the room. Since these lights are tungsten-balanced, you must use tungsten-balanced film. They provide the same flexibility as strobes, perhaps even more, because you can see the light

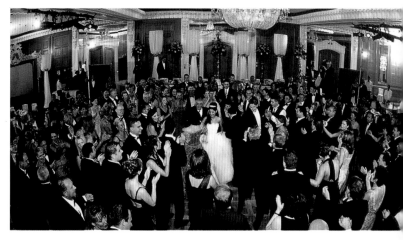

This is a dance floor at a wedding reception lit by quartz-halogen lights. You can see that there are a few "holes" in the lighting, but overall it's very even throughout. Since most of the activities happen in the center of the room, the lights are directed there. The photographer also used some of the tungsten-balanced stage lighting (see upper right-hand corner of the frame) for supplementary lighting. He then used the in-camera meter for all the exposures on the dance floor. Photograph by Vladimir Bekker.

falloff and, when shooting, you can use your in-camera meter for reliable results.

Whether you're using quartz lights or strobes in umbrellas, it is imperative to locate and secure the lights safely. Wedding receptions being sometimes raucous affairs, people could easily trip over the stands or any wires that are not completely taped down with duct tape. The last thing you want is for someone to be injured due to your carelessness.

○ Focusing Umbrellas

Umbrellas fit inside a tubular housing in most studio electronic flash units. The umbrella slides toward and away from the flash head and is anchored with a set-screw or similar device. The reason the umbrella-to-light-source distance is adjustable is that there is a set distance at which the full amount of strobe light hits the complete surface of the umbrella. This is optimal. If the umbrella is too close to the strobe, much of the beam of light is focused past the umbrella surface and goes to waste. When setting up, use the mod-

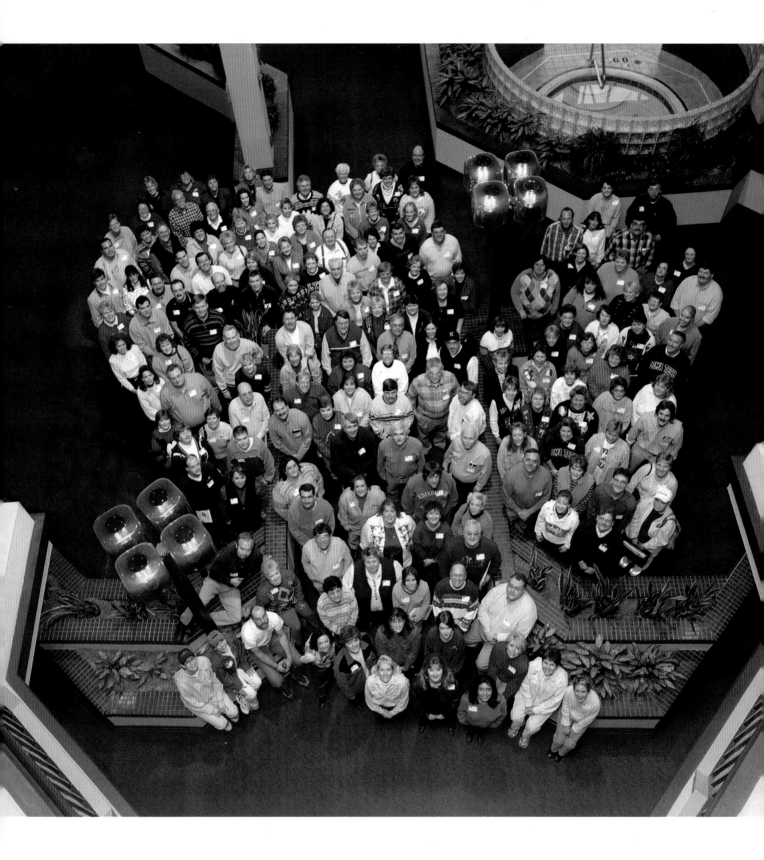

Opposite: Here's a bird's-eye view of a very large group. A high vantage point like this one is by far one of the best ways to photograph this many people. The photographer used multiple umbrellas to light the large group. The umbrellas were first focused and then feathered out to spread the light as evenly as possible. Meter readings were taken throughout the group to ensure even exposure. The light is soft and even throughout. Photograph by Michael Ayers. **Right:** *Window light is spectacular for small groups. Here, two young girls are positioned very close to the window light source with tight cropping. No fill-in source is needed because the light virtually wraps around the curved planes of their faces. Photograph by Norman Phillips.*

eling light of the strobe to focus the distance correctly, so the outer edges of the light core strike the outer edges of the umbrella for maximum light efficiency.

○ WINDOW LIGHT

One of the most flattering types of lighting you can use in group portraiture is window lighting. It is a soft light that minimizes facial imperfections, and is also a highly directional light, yielding good roundness and modeling qualities in portraits. Window light is usually a fairly bright light and it is infinitely variable, changing almost by the minute, allowing a great variety of moods in a single shooting session.

Window lighting has several drawbacks, as well. Since daylight falls off rapidly once it enters a window, and is much weaker several feet from the window than it is close to the window, great care must be taken in determining exposure, particularly with groups of three or four people. Another problem arises from shooting in buildings not designed for photography. You will sometimes have to work with distracting backgrounds and uncomfortably close shooting distances.

The best quality of window light is the soft light of mid-morning or mid-afternoon because it never gets direct sunlight. Direct sunlight is difficult to work with because of its intensity and because it will often create shadows of the individual windowpanes on the subject. It is often said that north light is the best for window-lit portraits. This is not necessarily true. Good quality light can be had from a window facing any direction, provided the light is soft.

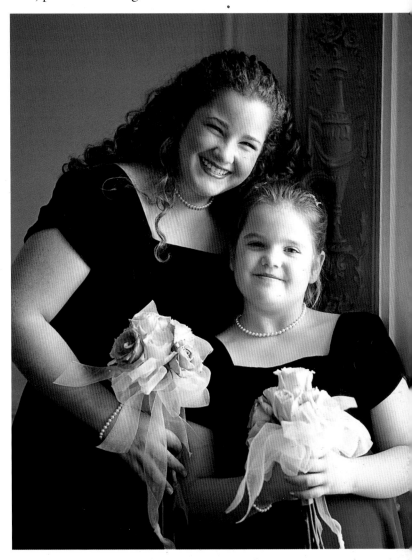

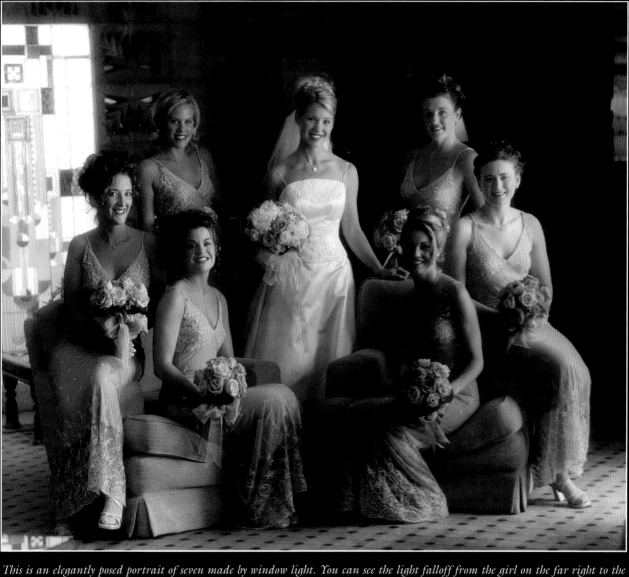

This is an elegantly posed portrait of seven made by window light. You can see the light falloff from the girl on the far right to the girl on the far left. The photographer based his exposure on the bride, who is beautifully lit from the side. The stained glass window at left is providing some much-needed fill light on the girls on the left of the frame. Note too that the girl on the left in the top row is leaning into the light. Photograph by Kenneth Sklute.

○ SUBJECT POSITIONING

One of the most difficult aspects of shooting window light portraits is positioning your subjects so that there is good facial modeling. If the subjects are placed parallel to the window, you will get a form of split lighting that can be harsh. It is best to position your subjects away from the window slightly so that they can look back toward the window. Thus, the lighting will highlight more area on the faces.

You can also position yourself between the window and your subjects for a flat type of lighting. Often, however, your figure will block much-needed light, or the subjects must be quite far

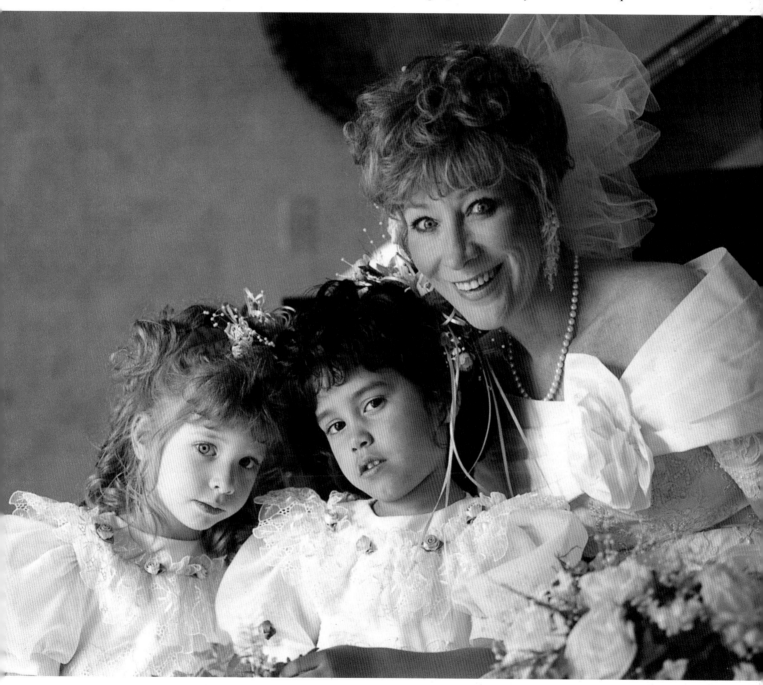

In this beautiful wedding image, window light was used to light this small group. Notice how tightly they are posed and also notice the light falloff that occurs from the little girl on the left to the bride. It falls off by about one f-stop in a span of approximately 14 inches. The fill was provided by light colored walls in the room. Photograph by Norman Phillips.

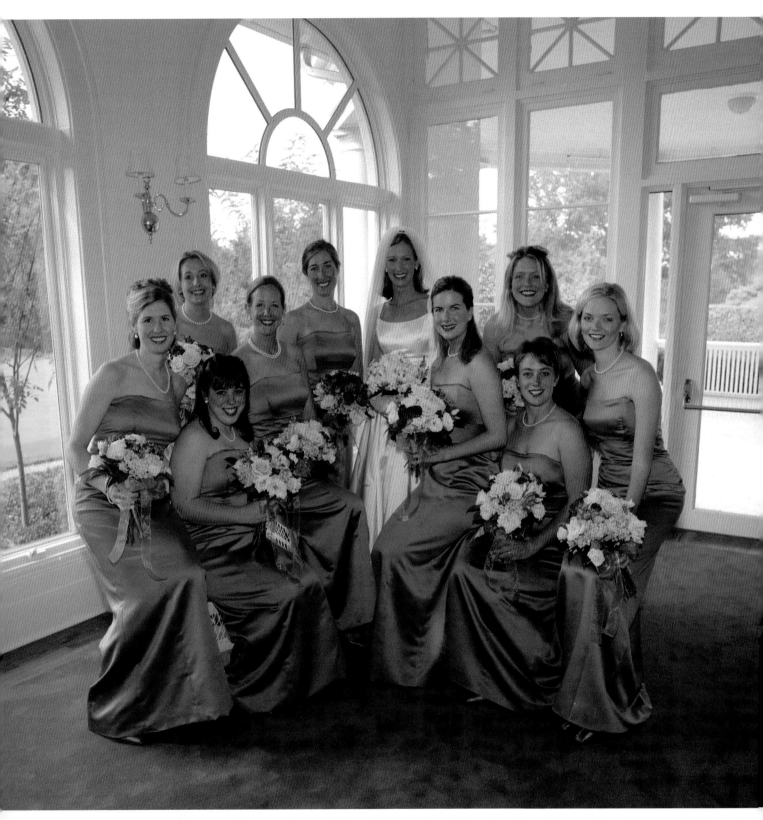

This is a portrait of the bridesmaids and bride with lots of pleasing triangle shapes throughout the composition. Wraparound windows created the main lighting and bounce flash from an umbrella-mounted strobe created the fill. The window light is soft and elegant, but without significant fill, the lighting would have a "hole," meaning there would be areas of underexposure in the middle of the group. The photographer read the exposure for the scene outside the room and matched his strobe output within a stop of the daylight exposure, for a balanced exposure inside and out. Photograph by Michael Ayers.

from the window to get proper perspective and composition. Under these circumstances, the light level will often be too low to make a decent exposure, even with fast film.

The light becomes more diffused the farther you move from the window.

The closer to the window your subjects are, the harsher the lighting will be. The light becomes more diffused the farther you move from the window. Usually, it is best to position the subjects 3–5 feet from the window. This not only gives better lighting, but gives you a little room to produce a flattering pose and pleasing composition.

○ EXPOSURE

The best way to meter for exposure is with a hand-held incident meter. Hold it in front of each of the subject's faces in the same light and take a reading, pointing the light-sensitive hemisphere directly at the camera lens. With more than one subject you'll get multiple readings. Choose an exposure midway between the two or three readings.

If using a reflected meter, like the in-camera meter, move in close and take readings off the faces. If the subjects are particularly fair-skinned, remember to open up at least one f-stop from the indicated reading. Most camera light meters take an average reading, so if you move in close on a person with an average skin tone, the meter will read the face, hair, and what little clothing and background it can see and give you a fairly good exposure reading. Average these readings and choose an intermediate exposure setting.

Since you will be using the lens at or near its widest aperture, it is important to focus carefully. Focus on the eyes and, if necessary, adjust members of the group forward or backward so they fall within the same focus plane. Depth of field is min-

imal at these apertures, so control the pose and focus as carefully as possible and be sure light falls evenly on all the faces.

○ FILL-IN ILLUMINATION

One of the biggest problems with window light is that there is not adequate fill light to illuminate the shadow side of the faces. The easiest way to fill the shadows is with a large white or silver fill reflector placed next to the subjects on the side opposite the window. The reflector has to be angled properly to direct the light back into the faces.

If you are shooting a ¾- or full-length portrait, a fill card may not be sufficient and it may be necessary to provide another source of illumination to achieve a good fill-in balance. Sometimes, if you flick on a few room lights, you will get good overall fill-in. Other times, you may have to use bounce flash.

If using the room lights for fill, be sure they do not overpower the window light, creating multiple lighting patterns. If the light is direct (casts its own set of noticeable shadows), then you are better off using another type of fill-in.

When using color film, you will get a warm glow from the tungsten room lights if you are using daylight-balanced film. This is not objectionable as long as the light is diffused and not too intense.

It is a good idea to have a room light in the background behind the subjects. This opens up an otherwise dark background and provides better depth in the portrait. If possible, position the background room light behind the subject, out of view of the camera, or off to the side, out of the camera's field of view so it lights the wall behind the subjects.

If none of the above methods of fill-in is available to you, use bounce flash. You can bounce the light from a portable electronic flash off a white card or the ceiling, or into an umbrella or a far wall, but be sure that it is one-half to one full f-stop less intense than the daylight. It is important

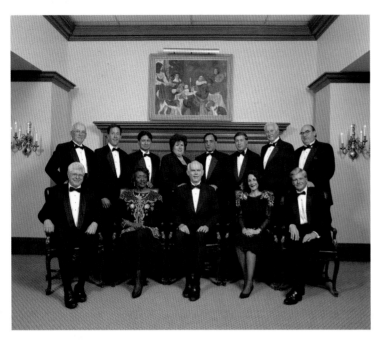

A formal group with a very structured pose but a very informal lighting technique—bounce flash off the ceiling. The photographer used two studio strobes on stands bounced off the ceiling near the camera and aimed at the group so that the lighting would be frontal but not too overhead in nature. Notice that the shadows are all tucked out of the way and the lighting is soft and even throughout. No retouching was required for this portrait and those wearing eyeglasses were rendered exceptionally well because of the bounce lighting. Photograph by Michael Ayers.

when using flash for fill-in to carry a flash meter for determining the intensity of the flash.

○ Diffusing Window Light

If you find a nice location for a portrait but the light coming through the windows is direct sunlight, you can diffuse the window light with some acetate diffusing material taped to the window frame. It produces a warm golden window light. Light diffused in this manner has the feeling of warm sunlight but without the harsh shadows. If still too harsh, try doubling the thickness of the acetate for more diffusion. When used on a movie set, these diffusers are called scrims. Since the light is so scattered by the scrim, you will probably not need a fill source, unless you are working with a larger group. In that case, use reflectors to reflect

light back into the faces of those farthest from the window.

○ Bounce Flash

Portable electronic flash is the most difficult of one-light applications. Portable flash units do not have modeling lights, so it is impossible to see the lighting effect. However, there are certain ways to use a portable flash in a predictable way to get excellent portrait lighting for groups.

Bounce flash is an ideal type of portrait light. It is soft and directional. By bouncing the flash off the ceiling or a side wall, you can achieve an elegant wraparound-style lighting that illuminates the subjects beautifully.

If you are using side-wall bounce flash, you will probably need to position a reflector at an angle to the group to kick in some much needed fill light.

You must learn to gauge angles when using bounce flash. Aim the flash unit at a point on the wall or ceiling that will produce the widest beam of light reflecting back onto your subjects.

You should never use color film when bouncing flash off colored walls. The light reflected back onto your subjects will be the same color as the walls or ceiling.

○ Lighting Large Groups with Bounce Flash

Michael Ayers, one of the featured photographers in this book, has several tips for lighting large groups. His recommendation is to use a white ceiling and bounce the flashes off the ceiling. "This gives a much more even lighting pattern. Also, aim to have a shallow lighting ratio for larger groups, like 1:1, 1:2 or 1:2.5, but never 1:4 or higher—the light is too hard to control. The quickest way to light a large group is to always utilize the ceiling. This is a perfect reflector or "umbrella," provided the ceiling is a shade of white. Bounce the light [from one or more studio strobes] from behind or beside the camera—many of our clients love the soft wraparound light pattern it creates for families and groups."

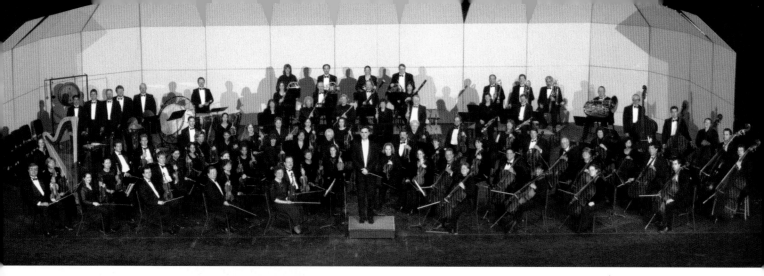

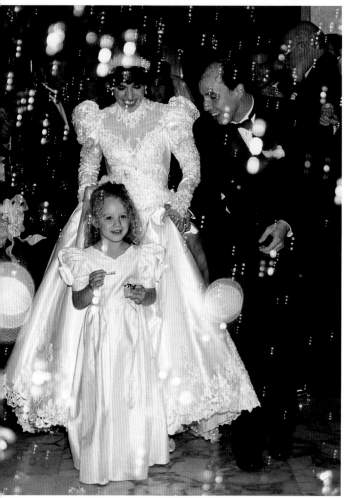

Above: *According to the photographer, this symphony photo would have looked better if he had placed the two fill lights on the sides of the camera (about 20 feet to either side) much higher. However, he could not raise them any higher in this auditorium. Also, he says, if he had used (or could find) two 20 x 20-foot softboxes to use (or 20-foot umbrellas) instead of the smaller reflectors on his lights, the shadows on the print would have been much softer. Considering the limitations, he did a pretty good job. Photograph by Michael Ayers.* **Left:** *This is perhaps the only "straight" flash image in this book. You can see why it's not favored for groups. Note the rapid light falloff and the sharpness of the light. However, straight flash also created the wonderful specular highlights on all those bubbles. And, it's a perfect exposure. Photograph by Andy Park.*

comes down) in order to properly set up bounce lights, particularly with strobes with minimal modeling lights. Choose the angle from the flash to the ceiling carefully, because the angle from the ceiling to the subject will be the same angle. Ayers cautions not to get the strobes too close to the group, otherwise you will produce an overhead type of lighting. With the right angle, bounce flash will eliminate the need for retouching. Its soft wraparound effect is ideal for medium to large size groups.

With quartz lights, which are extremely bright, you will be able to see the exact effect you will get, and meter it to make sure the lighting is even. Not true with strobes. You must set the lights carefully. A digital camera will allow you to preview the effectiveness of your lighting instantly.

The best means of determining exposure is with a flash meter. Use it at the group position to take readings at either end of the group and in the middle. You should not have more than one or two tenths of a stop difference between any of the readings.

You must determine the angle of incidence (what goes up) and the angle of reflection (what

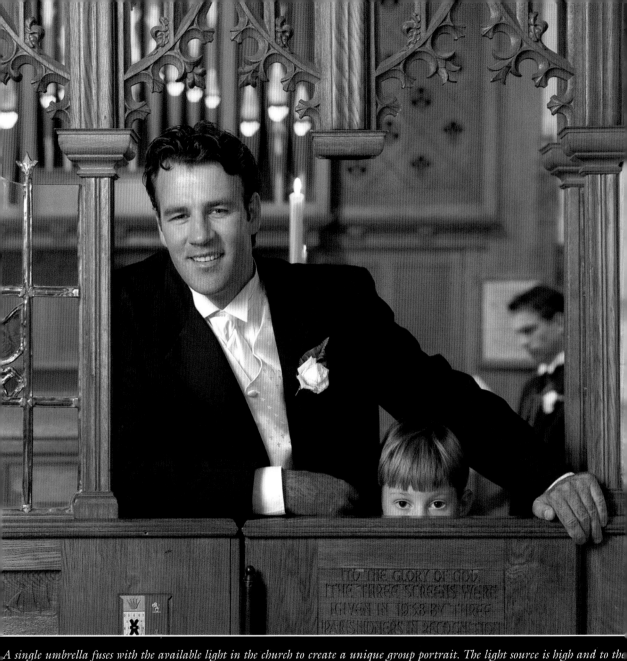

A single umbrella fuses with the available light in the church to create a unique group portrait. The light source is high and to the side, creating beautiful highlight brilliance and facial modeling. The light is also far enough to the side so that the grain of the wood is enhanced and the printing carved in the wood is completely readable. The design of the photo is such that the little boy (presumably the one with the cocktail earlier in this book) is just as important as the figure in the foreground and the one out of focus in the background. This image was part of a series done for Kodak Professional Australia. Photograph by David Anthony Williams.

DIFFUSED "STRAIGHT" FLASH

On-camera flash should be avoided altogether for making portraits unless it is a fill-in source. Its light is too harsh and flat and it produces no roundness or contouring of the faces. However, when you diffuse on-camera flash, you get a soft frontal lighting similar to fashion lighting. While diffused flash is still a flat lighting and frontal in nature, its softness produces much better contouring than direct undiffused flash.

There are various diffusers on the market that will diffuse on-camera flash. Most can even be used with your flash in auto or TTL mode, making exposure calculation effortless.

UMBRELLAS AND SOFTBOXES

Umbrellas and softboxes are ideal on-location lighting solutions for groups. A single softbox can be used for small groups to produce beautiful, in-studio lighting. Umbrellas can be used to light large areas for big groups.

Photographic umbrellas are either white or silvered. Softboxes are highly diffused and may even be double-diffused with the addition of a second scrim over the lighting surface. In addition, some softbox units accept multiple strobe heads for additional lighting power and intensity.

> Some umbrellas come with intermittent white and silvered panels.

A silver-lined umbrella produces a more specular, direct light than does a matte white umbrella. When using lights of equal intensity, a silver-lined umbrella can be used as a main light because of its increased intensity and directness. It will also produce wonderful specular highlights in the overall highlight areas of the face.

Some umbrellas come with intermittent white and silvered panels. These produce good overall soft light but with specular highlights. They are often called zebras.

Michael Ayers on Using Umbrellas. "When I first learned lighting from great photographers such as Bill Meriwether, Frank Cricchio, Don Blair, and Frank Kristian, they all emphasized the importance of using parabolic [row lighting in parabolic reflectors] lighting. They all played the same tune: 'If you can master parabolic lights, you can learn everything else.' They were right, and I recommend that students of photography begin their practice of forming and feathering light using parabolics first, before using umbrellas, barebulb flash, or softboxes.

"For many, umbrella lights are a favorite because they are light and compact, easy to use on location, can be feathered and adjusted precisely, and allow the photographer to utilize a broad light source with little effort.

"With translucent umbrellas, the light can be projected through the umbrella toward the subject instead of just reflecting the light off the back of the umbrella. In either case, 'focusing' the umbrella with the light source is important for proper control of the light. Many photographers mount the umbrella's shaft to the strobe at the end tip and point the shaft at the subject. This is incorrect. The modeling light must be turned on first, then the shaft needs to be moved in and out of the strobe until the light from the modeling bulb does not spill over the edges of the umbrella. Allowing light to fall over the edges can cause reflections, stray light, overexposure and unwanted highlights in the final image. Most strobe heads have, as an accessory, a very small diameter reflector that is to be used when using umbrellas. This device keeps stray light from spilling out of the light head and more evenly focuses the light into an umbrella or softbox.

"The other aspect of using umbrellas incorrectly is the problem of aiming the umbrella directly at the subject. Umbrellas have the ability to be feathered beautifully. The light from the edges of a correctly placed umbrella is usually the softest, whereas the light from the center often has a hot spot. Using a light meter to find the broad, smooth light along the edge of an umbrella is the best operation to perform before making any exposures."

○ THE MAKING OF THE ULTIMATE GROUP SHOT

The United Nations Millennium Conference, the largest gathering in the history of world leaders, brought together 189 heads of government and high-ranking officials from around the world. A top-notch photo team recruited by Eastman Kodak Company made the ultimate group photograph. The photo, commissioned by the United Nations, appeared in major magazines and newspapers throughout the world.

The team of photographers was put together by Terry Deglau, then the manager of trade relations at Eastman Kodak. The photographers and three camera formats were chosen for the job: Bob Golding would shoot the 4x5s, Tony Corbell

would shoot the medium format images on a Hasselblad and Rick Billings, who shot with a Kodak DCS 560 digital camera, would produce the photos for worldwide distribution to the news media.

A large portion of the success of this venture would depend on good lighting. The team used four 1000 watt-second Photogenic strobes with parabolic reflectors at the camera position. Another four Photogenic strobes were used on stands with umbrellas closer to the group, and two more strobes were used for separation lights. The lights, once set, produced an f/22 exposure with no more than $\frac{1}{10}$ stop deviation across the entire group area.

To give each dignitary his or her own space, Deglau planned on giving each person 18 inches of room, shoulder to shoulder. Because of perspective, the shot required that there be fewer people in the front row than in the back. Deglau's calculations put nineteen in the first row and

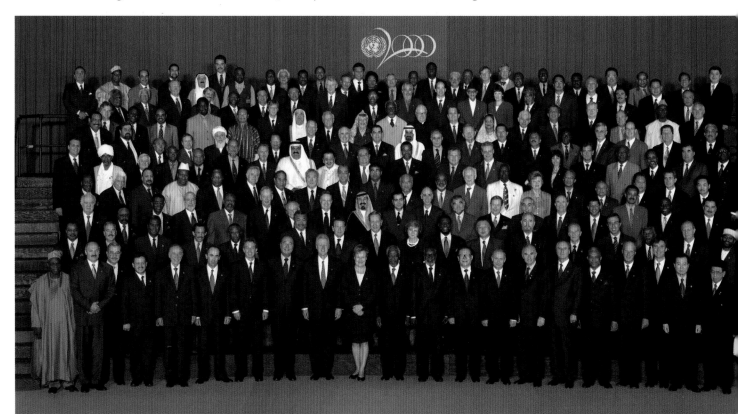

UN photo by Terry Deglau for Eastman Kodak Company, September 2000.

twenty-five in the back row so that the final composition would build straight lines on the left and right.

Two scaffoldings were erected, one 16 feet off the ground, the other 11. The higher of the two held the three photographers, the shorter one was for Deglau, who was miked to address the group.

Risers were built with a one-foot rise and, to ensure that every face would be clearly visible, every other row was moved nine inches to the right. Paper footprints were taped onto the floor, each having the dignitary's name and country written on them. All of the dignitaries were then given pieces of paper to identify their exact location.

How did they get the great exposure? Deglau, who was positioned in front of the three photographers, explained to the dignitaries that, "In America, photographers may count to three and make an exposure." He then said, "Let's try it!" The photographers had planned to make the exposure when the group looked good and was paying attention. It came after the count of "two." Deglau pointed to the photographers behind him and said to the group, "they can't count." The group laughed and they made a second exposure, which was the best expression.

If you're thinking a shot like this couldn't have gone that smoothly, you're right.

If you're thinking a shot like this couldn't have gone that smoothly, you're right. The dignitary in the gold robe at the far left of the first row would simply not move closer to the group. He steadfastly stayed two feet or more from the person next to him. Deglau, who had been instructed not to touch any of the dignitaries, went to the man's location and tried to get him to move over, even going so far as to give him a gentle nudge. The man completely ignored Terry and looked at him as if he didn't understand a word of English. Deglau went back to his platform and the shot proceeded. In the end, Rick Billings, who had made the digital images of the group, "moved" the man over digitally, tucking him in behind the shoulder of the man on his left.

Only thirty minutes had been allotted to make this momentous photograph. In fact, fifteen exposures were made on the three different cameras in just twenty-three minutes. That's the total elapsed time from the time the group arrived to the completion of the photography. The team had eight good exposures to choose from.

At the conclusion of the photography session, the presidents and dignitaries gave Deglau and the team a warm round of applause for the excellent event planning.

Several days later, 16x20 prints framed and matted by Art Leather/GNP were signed by the Secretary-General of the UN and given to each of the heads of state as a gift for attending the UN conference.

GLOSSARY

Barn doors. Black, metal folding doors that attach to a light's reflector. These are used to control the width of the beam of light.

Box light. A diffused light source housed in a box-shaped reflector. The bottom of the box is translucent material; the side pieces of the box are opaque, but they are coated with a reflective material such as foil on the inside to optimize light output.

Bounce flash. Bouncing the light of a studio or portable flash off a surface such as a ceiling or wall to produce indirect, shadowless lighting.

Burning-in. A darkroom printing technique in which specific areas of the print surface are given additional exposure in order to darken them.

Catchlight. The specular highlights that appear in the iris or pupil of the subject's eyes, reflected from the portrait lights.

CC filters. Color compensating filters that come in gel or glass form and are used to correct the color balance of a scene.

Color temperature. The degrees Kelvin of a light source. Also refers to a film's sensitivity. Color films are balanced for 5500°K (daylight), or 3200°K (tungsten) or 3400°K (photoflood).

Cross lighting. Lighting that comes from the side of the subject, skimming facial surfaces to reveal the maximum texture in the skin. Also called sidelighting.

Cross shadows. Shadows created by lighting a group with two light sources from either side of the camera. These should be eliminated to restore the "one-light" look.

Depth of field. The distance that is sharp beyond and in front of the focus point at a given f-stop.

Depth of focus. The amount of sharpness that extends in front of and behind the focus point. The depth of focus of some lenses extends 50 percent in front of and 50 percent behind the focus point. Other lenses may vary.

Dodging. Darkroom printing technique in which specific areas of the print are given less print exposure by blocking the light to those areas of the print, making those areas lighter.

Dope. Retouching medium that is often applied to negatives to give them a suitable retouching surface, or "tooth."

Dragging the shutter. Using a shutter speed slower than the X sync speed in order to capture the ambient light in a scene.

E.I. Otherwise known as exposure index. The term refers to a film speed other than the rated ISO of the film.

Feathering. Misdirecting the light deliberately so that the edge of the beam of light illuminates the subject.

Fill card. A white or silver-foil-covered card used to reflect light back into the shadow areas of the subject.

Fill light. Secondary light source used to fill in the shadows created by the key light.

Flash fill. Flash technique that uses electronic flash to fill in the shadows created by the main light source.

Flashing. A technique used in printing to darken an area of the print by exposing it to raw light.

Flash key. Flash technique in which the flash becomes the main light source and the ambient light in the scene fills the shadows created by the flash.

Foreshortening. A distortion of normal perspective caused by close proximity of the camera/lens to the subject. Foreshortening exaggerates subject features—noses appear elongated, chins jut out and the backs of heads may appear smaller than normal.

45-degree lighting. Portrait lighting pattern characterized by a triangular highlight on the shadow side of the face. Also known as Rembrandt lighting.

Focusing an umbrella. Adjusting the length of the exposed shaft of an umbrella in a light housing to optimize light output.

Full-length portrait. A pose that includes the full figure of the model. Full-length portraits can show the subject standing, seated or reclining.

Gobo. Light-blocking card that is supported on a stand or boom and positioned between the light source and subject to selectively block light from portions of the scene.

Golden mean. A rule of composition that gives a guideline for the most dynamic area in which to place the subject. Determined by drawing a diagonal line from one corner of the frame to the other, then drawing a line from either remaining corner of the frame so that the diagonal is intersected perpendicularly.

Groundglass. The camera's focusing screen on which the image is focused.

Head-and-shoulder axis. Imaginary lines running through shoulders (shoulder axis) and down the ridge of the nose (head axis). Head-and-shoulder axes should never be perpendicular to the line of the lens axis.

High-key lighting. Type of lighting characterized by low lighting ratio and a predominance of light tones.

Highlight brilliance. Refers to the specularity of highlights on the skin. A negative with good highlight brilliance shows specular highlights (paper base white) within a major highlight area. Achieved through good lighting and exposure techniques.

Key light. The main light in portraiture used to establish the lighting pattern and define the facial features of the subject.

Kicker. A backlight (a light coming from behind the subject) that highlights the hair or contour of the body.

Lead-in line. In compositions, a pleasing line in the scene that leads the viewer's eye toward the main subject.

Lighting ratio. The difference in intensity between the highlight side of the face and the shadow side of the face. A 3:1 ratio implies that the highlight side is three times brighter than the shadow side of the face.

Loop lighting. A portrait lighting pattern characterized by a loop-like shadow on the shadow side of the subject's face. Differs from paramount or butterfly lighting because the main light is slightly lower and farther to the side of the subject.

Low-key lighting. Type of lighting characterized by a high lighting ratio and strong scene contrast as well as a predominance of dark tones.

Main light. Synonymous with key light.

Matte box. A front-lens accessory with retractable bellows that holds filters, masks and vignettes for modifying the image.

Modeling light. A secondary light mounted in the center of a studio flash head that gives a close approximation of the lighting that the flash tube will produce. Usually high intensity, low-heat output quartz bulbs.

Optimum lens aperture. The aperture on a lens that produces the sharpest image. It is usually two stops down from the widest aperture. If the lens is an f/2.8 lens, for example, the optimum aperture would be f/5.6.

Paramount lighting. One of the basic portrait lighting patterns, characterized by a high-key light placed directly in line with the line of the subject's nose. This lighting produces a butterfly-like shadow under the nose. Also called butterfly lighting.

Perspective. The appearance of objects in a scene as determined by their relative distance and position.

Reflector. (1) Same as fill card. (2) A housing on a light that reflects the light outward in a controlled beam.

Rembrandt lighting. Same as 45-degree lighting.

Rim lighting. Portrait lighting pattern where the key light is behind the subject and illuminates the edge of the subject. Most often used with profile poses.

Rule of thirds. Format for composition that divides the image area into thirds, horizontally and vertically. The intersection of two lines is a dynamic point where the subject should be placed for the most visual impact.

⅞ view. Facial pose that shows approximately ⅞ of the face. Almost a full-face view as seen from the camera.

Scrim. A panel used to diffuse sunlight. Scrims can be mounted in panels and set in windows, used on stands, or they can be suspended in front of a light source to diffuse the light.

Softbox. Same as a box light. Can contain one or more light heads and single or double-diffused scrims.

Soft-focus lens. Special lens that uses spherical or chromatic aberration in its design to diffuse the image points.

Specular highlights. Sharp, dense image points on the negative. Specular highlights are very small and usually appear on pores in the skin. Specular highlights are pure white with no detail.

Split lighting. Type of portrait lighting that splits the face into two distinct areas: shadow side and highlight side. The key light is placed far to the side of the subject and slightly higher than the subject's head height.

Straight flash. The light of an on-camera flash unit that is used without diffusion; i.e., straight.

Swings and tilts. View camera movements of the lens and film stages. Used to correct perspective and control the plane of focus.

TTL-balanced fill-flash. Flash exposure systems that read the flash exposure through the camera lens and adjust flash output to compensate for flash and ambient light exposures, producing a balanced exposure.

Tension. A state of visual imbalance within a photograph.

¾-length pose. Pose that includes all but the lower portion of the subject's anatomy. Can be from above knees and up, or below knees and up.

¾ view. Facial pose that allows the camera to see ¾ of the facial area. Subject's face usually turned 45 degrees away from the lens so that the far ear disappears from camera view.

Tooth. Refers to a negative that has a built-in retouching surface that will accept retouching leads.

Umbrella lighting. Type of soft, casual lighting that uses one or more photographic umbrellas to diffuse the light source(s).

Vignette. A semicircular, soft-edged border around the main subject. Vignettes can be either light or dark in tone and can be included at the time of shooting, or added later in printing.

Wraparound lighting. Soft type of light, produced by umbrellas, that wraps around the subject, producing a low lighting ratio and open, well-illuminated highlight areas.

X sync. The shutter speed at which focal-plane shutters synchronize with electronic flash.

Zebra. A term used to describe reflectors or umbrellas having alternating reflecting materials such as silver and white cloth.

CONTRIBUTING PHOTOGRAPHERS

J. J. Allen. J. J. Allen of Hapeville, Georgia, has been a photographer for over fifty years. He is the author of *Posing and Lighting Techniques for Studio Portrait Photography* (Amherst Media) and a book dealing with .on-location portraiture, forthcoming from Amherst Media.

Michael J. Ayers, PPA-Certified, M.Photog., Cr., APM, AOPA, AEPA, AHPA. WPPI's 1997 International Portrait Photographer of the Year, Michael Ayers, is a studio owner from Lima, Ohio. He has lectured to other photographers about portraiture and his "Album Architecture" all across North America and he has been a featured speaker in Europe.

Vladimir Bekker. Vladimir Bekker, owner of Concord Photography in Toronto, Canada, specializes in weddings and environmental portraits. An immigrant from the Ukraine, Vladimir took up photography when he was a boy. He is a graduate of Lvov Polytechnical University with a master's degree in architecture, which explains why many of his wedding images include architectural details. His studio photographs over 100 weddings a year. He has won numerous international awards for his prints and albums.

David Bentley, M.Photog.,Cr. David Bentley owns and operates Bentley Studio, Ltd. in Frontenac, Missouri with his wife Susan, also a master photographer. With a background in engineering, he calls upon a systematic as well as creative approach to each of his assignments. His thirty years of experience and numerous awards speak to the success of the system.

Anthony Cava, BA, MPA, APPO. Born and raised in Ottawa, Ontario, Canada, Anthony Cava owns and operates Photolux Studio with his brother, Frank. Frank and Anthony's parents originally founded Photolux as a wedding/portrait studio, thirty years ago. Anthony joined WPPI and the Professional Photographers of Canada ten years ago. At thirty years old, he is the youngest "Master of Photographic Arts" (MPA) in Canada. Cava won WPPI's Grand Award for the year with the first print that he ever entered in competition.

Stephen Dantzig, Psy.D. Dr. Stephen Dantzig owns and operates a small commercial studio just north of Los Angeles. His work ranges from commercial fashion to products and interiors to executive portraits.

Terry Deglau. Terry Deglau has been a professional portrait photographer for over forty years. He is the former manager of trade relations at Eastman Kodak Company. Terry is a Rochester Institute of Technology graduate with a degree in Photographic Science and a marketing degree from the University of Pittsburgh. Terry and friends have lectured extensively throughout the US and the world.

William L. Duncan, M.Photog., CPP, APM, AOPM, AEPA. Bill Duncan was one of the original members of WPPI with three levels of advancement. He has been a consistent winner in print competitions from all organizations and he is known around the country for his unique and stylized images. He is the instructor of the "Artistry In the Language of Light" seminars.

Gary Fagan, M.Photog.,Cr., CPP. Gary, along with his wife Jan, owns and operates an in-home studio in Dubuque, Iowa. Gary concentrates primarily on families and high-school seniors, using his half-acre outdoor studio as the main setting. At a recent WPPI convention, Gary was awarded WPPI's Accolade of Lifetime Excellence. He was also awarded the International Portrait of the year by that same organization. At the Heart of America convention, he had the Top Master Print and the Best of Show. For the highest master print in the region, Gary received the Regional Gold Medallion award at the PPA national convention ASP banquet.

Rick Ferro, Certified Professional Photographer. Rick Ferro has served as senior wedding photographer at Walt Disney World. In his twenty years of photography experience, he has photographed over 10,000 weddings. He has received numerous awards, including having prints accepted into PPA's Permanent Loan Collection. He has won numerous awards from WPPI and he is the author of *Wedding Photography: Creative Techniques for Lighting and Posing* (Second Edition), published by Amherst Media.

Frank A. Frost, Jr., PPA-Certified, M.Photog.,Cr., APM, AOPA. AEPA. AHPA. Located in the heart of the Southwest, Frank Frost has been creating his own classic portraiture in Albuquerque, New Mexico for over eighteen years. Believing that "success is in the details," Frank pursues both the artistry and business of photography with remarkable results, earning him numerous awards from WPPI and PPA along the way. His photographic ability stems from an instinctive flair for posing, composition and lighting.

Dale P. Hansen, PPA Cert., APM, AOPA Dale Hansen holds a BA degree from Brooks Institute of Photography in Santa Barbara, California and has had many of his photographs published nationally, in such publications as *Audubon, National Geographic, World Book* and the cover of *PPA Storyteller* in March 1999.

Robert L. Kunesh, PPA Cert., M.Photog., CPP, AOPM. Robert Kunesh has been a professional photographer since 1967. From 1961 until his retirement in 1991, he taught art and graphic arts in various Ohio schools. In 1967, he began photographing weddings for a studio in Cleveland. He has now photographed over 1000 weddings. Since 1986 he has been a co-owner of Studio K Photography and SKP Photo Lab in Willoughby, Ohio. Bob has received numerous awards including a Kodak Gallery award, three PPA Loan Images, and most recently, WPPI's Accolades of Photographic Mastery and Outstanding Achievement, as well as PPA Certification and Master of Photography degrees.

Robert Lino, M.Photog.,Cr., PAPM, AOPM, AEPA, FDPE, FSA. Robert Lino of Miami, Florida specializes in fine portraiture and social events. His style is formal and elegant, excelling in stylized poses. His ability to capture feeling and emotion in every image is unparalleled. Lino is a highly decorated photographer in national and international print competitions and is a regular on the workshop and seminar circuit.

Robert Love, APM, AOPA, AEPA, M.Photog.,Cr., CPP and Suzanne Love, Cr. Photog. Robert Love is a member of Camera-craftsmen of America, one of forty active members in the world. He and his wife, Suzanne, create all of their images on location. Preferring the early evening "love light," they have claimed the outdoors as their "studio." This gives their images a feeling of romance and tranquillity.

Heidi Mauracher, M.Photog.,Cr., CPP, FBIPP, AOPA, AEPA, F-ASP. Heidi Mauracher has presented programs before audiences around the world. She has taught at several affiliated schools as well as the PPA's Winona School of Professional Photography. Her articles and photographic images have been featured in a variety of professional magazines and books, and her unique style has won her many PPA Loan Collection prints and more than one photograph that has scored a perfect 100 in international competition.

William S. McIntosh, M.Photog.,Cr., F-ASP. Bill McIntosh photographs executives and their families all over the US and travels to England frequently on special assignments. He has lectured all over the world. His popular book, *Location Portraiture: The Story Behind the Art* (Tiffen Company LLC, 1996), is sold in bookstores and other outlets around the country.

Andy Park. Andy Park is a San Rafael, California-based wedding photographer who operates a unique "Internet-only" business. His web site, www.andypark.com, attracts business from all over the world. Park is a former newspaperman and radio and TV newsperson who became a wedding photographer in 1991.

Richard Pahl. Richard Pahl first gained recognition in his early twenties, scoring a first and second in a municipal photo contest. Several years ago, he began winning major competitions for professional photographers. Several of his images have been accepted in the PPA Loan Collection. He has scored two perfect 100s and won a Grand Award in Wedding and Portrait Photographers International competitions.

Norman Phillips, AOPA. Norman Phillips has been awarded the WPPI Accolade of Outstanding Photographic Achievement (AOPA), is a registered Master Photographer with Britain's Master Photographers Association, is a Fellow of the Society of Wedding & Portrait Photographers, and a Technical Fellow of Chicagoland Professional Photographers Association. He is a frequent contributor to photographic publications, a print judge and a guest speaker at seminars and workshops across the country.

Stephen Pugh. Stephen Pugh is an award-winning wedding photographer from Great Britain. He is a competing member of both WPPI and the British Guild and has won numerous awards in international print competitions.

Patrick Rice, M.Photog.Cr., CPP, AHPA. Patrick Rice is an award-winning portrait and wedding photographer with over twenty years in the profession. A popular author, lecturer and judge, he presents programs to photographers across the United States and Canada.

Kimarie Richardson. Kimarie Richardson owns and operates Fantasy Stills by Kimarie in Ukiah, California. She is a professionally trained makeup artist and a self-taught photographer, who made the transition to full-time photography ten years ago. She is well known in the Northern California area, and more recently nationally, for her hand-painted Angel Baby portraits, children's portraits, and Hollywood '40s-style glamour photographs. Two years ago she entered an international print competition for the first time and won a Grand Award for her print, "Angelica's Light."

Kenneth Sklute. Beginning his wedding photography career at the age of sixteen in Long Island, New York, Kenneth quickly advanced to shooting an average of 150 weddings a year. He purchased his first studio in 1984 and soon after received his Masters degree from PPA in 1986. In 1996, he moved to Arizona, where he enjoys a thriving business. Kenneth is much decorated, having been named Long Island Wedding Photographer of the Year fourteen times, PPPA Photographer of the Year and APPA Wedding Photographer of the Year. He has won these awards numerous times as well as winning numerous Fuji Masterpiece Awards and Kodak Gallery Awards.

David Anthony Williams, M.Photog., FRPS David Anthony Williams owns and operates a wedding studio in Ashburton, Victoria, Australia. In 1992 he achieved the rare distinction of Associateship and Fellowship of the Royal Photographic Society of Great Britain (FRPS) on the same day. Through the annual Australian Professional Photography Awards system, Williams achieved the level of Master of Photography with Gold Bar—the equivalent of a double master. In 2000, he was awarded the Accolade of Outstanding Photographic Achievement from WPPI, and has been a Grand Award winner at their annual conventions in both 1997 and 2000.

Monte Zucker. When it comes to perfection in posing and lighting, timeless imagery and contemporary, yet classical photographs, Monte Zucker is world famous. He's been bestowed every major honor the photographic profession can offer, including WPPI's Lifetime Achievement Award. In his endeavor to educate photographers at the highest level, Monte, along with partner Gary Bernstein, has created an information-based web site for photographers, Zuga.net.

ABOUT THE AUTHOR

Bill Hurter is the editor of *Rangefinder* magazine, a monthly publication for professional photographers. He is the former editor of *Petersen's PhotoGraphic* magazine and a graduate of Brooks Institute of Photography, from which he holds a BFA in professional photography and an honorary Masters of Science degree. He has been involved in professional photography for more than twenty-five years.

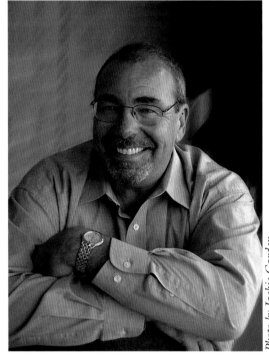

Photo by Jackie Carden

INDEX

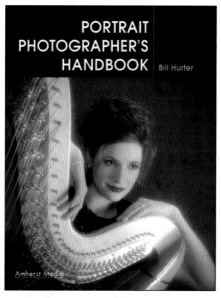

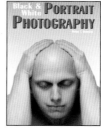
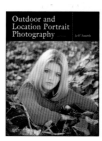
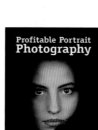
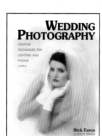
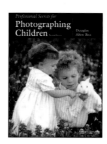

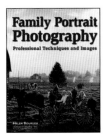

Family Portrait Photography

Helen Boursier

Learn from professionals how to operate a successful portrait studio. Includes: marketing family portraits, advertising, working with clients, posing, lighting, and selection of equipment. Includes images from a variety of top portrait shooters. $29.95 list, 8½x11, 120p, 123 photos, index, order no. 1629.

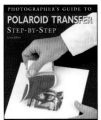

Photographer's Guide to Polaroid Transfer
2nd Edition

Christopher Grey

Step-by-step instructions make it easy to master Polaroid transfer and emulsion lift-off techniques and add new dimensions to your photographic imaging. Fully illustrated every step of the way to ensure good results the very first time! $29.95 list, 8½x11, 128p, 50 full-color photos, order no. 1653.

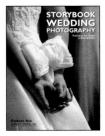

Storytelling Wedding Photography

Barbara Box

Barbara and her husband shoot as a team at weddings. Here, she shows you how to create outstanding candids (which are her specialty), and combine them with formal portraits (her husband's specialty) to create a unique wedding album. $29.95 list, 8½x11, 128p, 60 b&w photos, order no. 1667.

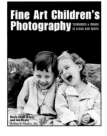

Fine Art Children's Photography

Doris Carol Doyle and Ian Doyle

Learn to create fine art portraits of children in black & white. Included is information on: posing, lighting for studio portraits, shooting on location, clothing selection, working with kids and parents, and much more! $29.95 list, 8½x11, 128p, 60 photos, order no. 1668.

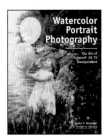

Watercolor Portrait Photography
THE ART OF
POLAROID SX-70 MANIPULATION

Helen T. Boursier

Create one-of-a-kind images with this surprisingly easy artistic technique. $29.95 list, 8½x11, 128p, 200+ color photos, order no. 1698.

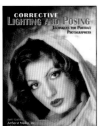

Corrective Lighting and Posing Techniques for Portrait Photographers

Jeff Smith

Learn to make every client look his or her best by using lighting and posing to conceal real or imagined flaws—from baldness, to acne, to figure flaws. $29.95 list, 8½x11, 120p, full color, 150 photos, order no. 1711.

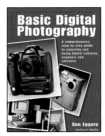

Basic Digital Photography

Ron Eggers

Step-by-step text and clear explanations teach you how to select and use all types of digital cameras. Learn all the basics with no-nonsense, easy to follow text designed to bring even true novices up to speed quickly and easily. $17.95 list, 8½x11, 80p, 40 b&w photos, order no. 1701.

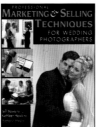

Professional Marketing & Selling Techniques for Wedding Photographers

Jeff Hawkins and Kathleen Hawkins

Learn the business of successful wedding photography. Includes consultations, direct mail, print advertising, internet marketing and much more. $29.95 list, 8½x11, 128p, 80 photos, order no. 1712.

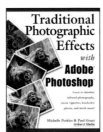

Traditional Photographic Effects with Adobe Photoshop

Michelle Perkins and Paul Grant

Use Photoshop to enhance your photos with handcoloring, vignettes, soft focus and much more. Every technique contains step-by-step instructions for easy learning. $29.95 list, 8½x11, 128p, 150 photos, order no. 1721.

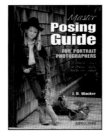

Master Posing Guide for Portrait Photographers

J. D. Wacker

Learn the techniques you need to pose single portrait subjects, couples and groups for studio or location portraits. Includes techniques for photographing weddings, teams, children, special events and much more. $29.95 list, 8½x11, 128p, 80 photos, order no. 1722.

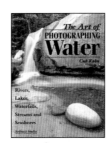

The Art of Photographing Water
RIVERS, LAKES, WATERFALLS
STREAMS & SEASHORES

Cub Kahn

Learn to capture the dynamic interplay of light and water with this beautiful, compelling and comprehensive book. $29.95 list, 8½x11, 128p, 70 full-color photos, order no. 1724.

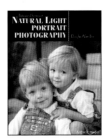

Professional Secrets of Natural Light Portrait Photography

Douglas Allen Box

Learn to utilize natural light to create inexpensive and hassle-free portraiture. Beautifully illustrated with detailed instructions on equipment, setting selection and posing. $29.95 list, 8½x11, 128p, 80 full-color photos, order no. 1706.

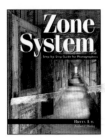

Zone System
STEP-BY-STEP GUIDE FOR
PHOTOGRAPHERS

Brian La

Learn to create perfectly exposed black & white negatives and top-quality prints. With this guide anyone can learn the Zone System! $29.95 list, 8½x11, 128p, 70 photos, order no. 1720.

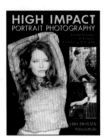

High Impact Portrait Photography
CREATIVE TECHNIQUES FOR
DRAMATIC, FASHION-INSPIRED
PORTRAITS

Lori Brystan

Learn how to create the high-end, fashion-inspired portraits your clients will love. Features posing, alternative processing and much more. $29.95 list, 8½x11, 128p, 60 full-color photos, order no.

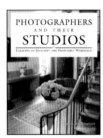

Photographers and Their Studios
CREATING AN EFFICIENT AND
PROFITABLE WORKSPACE

Helen T. Boursier

Tour the studios of working professionals, and learn their creative solutions for common problems, as well as how they optimized their studios for maximum sales. $29.95 list, 8½x11, 128p, 100 photos, order no. 1713.

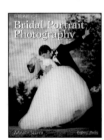

The Art of Bridal Portrait Photography
TECHNIQUES FOR
LIGHTING AND POSING

Marty Seefer

Learn to give every client your best and create timeless images that are sure to become family heirlooms. Seefer takes readers through every step of the bridal shoot, ensuring flawless results. $29.95 list, 8½x11, 128p, 70 full-color photos, order no. 1730.

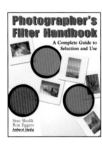

Photographer's Filter Handbook
A COMPLETE GUIDE TO
SELECTION AND USE

Stan Sholik and Ron Eggers

Take control of your photography with the tips offered in this book! This comprehensive volume teaches readers how to color-balance images, correct contrast problems, create special effects and more. $29.95 list, 8½x11, 128p, 100 full-color photos, order no. 1731.

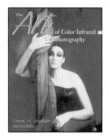

The Art of Color Infrared Photography
Steven H. Begleiter

Color infrared photography will open the doors to an entirely new and exciting photographic world. This exhaustive book shows readers how to previsualize the scene and get the results they want. $29.95 list, 8½x11, 128p, 80 full-color photos, order no. 1728.

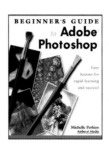

Beginner's Guide to Adobe® Photoshop®
EASY LESSONS FOR
RAPID LEARNING AND SUCCESS!

Michelle Perkins

Learn the skills you need to effectively make your images look their best, create original artwork or add unique effects to almost image. All topics are presented in short, easy-to-digest sections that will boost confidence and ensure outstanding images. $29.95 list, 8½x11, 128p, 150 full-color photos, order no. 1732.

More Photo Books Are Available

Contact us for a FREE catalog:
AMHERST MEDIA
PO BOX 586
AMHERST, NY 14226 USA

www.AmherstMedia.com

Ordering & Sales Information:

INDIVIDUALS: If possible, purchase books from an Amherst Media retailer. Write to us for the dealer nearest you. To order direct, send a check or money order with a note listing the books you want and your shipping address. For U.S. delivery, freight charges for first book are $4.00 (add $1.00 for each additional book). For delivery to Canada/Mexico, freight charges for first book are $9.00 (add $2.50 for each additional book). For delivery to all other countries, freight charges for first book are $11.00 (add $2.50 for each additional book). Visa and MasterCard accepted. New York state residents add 8% sales tax.

DEALERS, DISTRIBUTORS & COLLEGES: Write, call or fax to place orders. For price information, contact Amherst Media or an Amherst Media sales representative. Net 30 days.

1(800)622-3278 or (716)874-4450
FAX: (716)874-4508

All prices, publication dates, and specifications are subject to change without notice.
Prices are in U.S. dollars. Payment in U.S. funds only.